'*The Money Train* is the roadmap to a goldmine; David Pattison spills the secrets that are normally kept to exclusive networks or charged for six-figure fees. Set to be *the* essential guide for entrepreneurs who want to take their business to the next level.'

Bruce Daisley – author of the No.1 Sunday Times Business Bestseller *30 Ways to Fix Your Work Culture and Fall in Love with Your Job Again*

'This is a brilliantly practical, well-structured book written by someone who has the experience and wisdom to share his knowledge. It doesn't preach or lecture but has golden insights into the pitfalls and opportunities young businesses face from someone who has witnessed first-hand huge highs and some lows. Every young business and entrepreneur should make this their handbook.'

Dame Carolyn McCall – CEO, ITV plc

'Spending time with David is always time well spent and this book is no exception. What I appreciate the most about David is his razor-sharp questions and practical insights. Reading this book was the same as every conversation I've had with David, he's supportive but there's no sugar-coating, and for any business considering investment this is a must-read'.

Sarah Ellis – author of the No.1 Sunday Times Business Bestseller *The Squiggly Career* and Co-Founder, Amazing If

'I have been a business founder and an investor. I have built businesses from scratch and inherited large organizations. I have worked alone and in partnerships. I have used my own capital as well as having investors both private and institutional.

This book takes me back to the early days of being a founder. It made me smile at the memories of some of the situations David describes. His insights and advice are spot on and will help any young business founder to navigate the shark-infested waters of the

investment world. He charts the positives and pitfalls of taking outside investment. Either way, *The Money Train* is essential reading for any young entrepreneur.'

Steve Parish – Chairman, Crystal Palace Football Club, business founder and investor

'Forget theory, this is entrepreneurship told as real-world life experience – one that every entrepreneur, myself included, can instantly recognize. With this book, David has mapped your uncharted territory for you. Take it on your journey.'

Mark Eaves – Founder, Gravity Road

'An excellent read, with an easy layout and flow. This book is refreshingly honest and practical for an up and coming entrepreneur or someone raising money. I wish it had been around when we first started our fund-raising processes! David's experience is clearly demonstrated throughout, highlighting so many of the potential wins and pitfalls, needle moving details and levers that are critical in making a fundraise a success. Highly recommend.'

Dominic Joseph – Founder, Captify

'*The Money Train* is not only a great read, but also a fantastic reference book for founders when it comes to fundraising. It provides reassurance on the things you're doing right, as well as guidance on areas that need improvement. I can say this first-hand, as it's exactly how I use it.'

Paul Grundy – Founder, Baggl

'Be prepared, you will have David Pattison's voice permanently in your head when you start reading this book. He has managed to read your thoughts, capture your questions, your fears, your hopes, compiled them and answered them comprehensively and compassionately. (He never makes you feel stupid for not knowing what you don't know.) Your Money Train will feel and run more smoothly because this book exists.'

Muna Nageh – Founder, The Circle of Style

'*The Money Train* is an incredibly insightful yet easy read which I'd recommend to anyone going through or thinking about raising investment. The tone is spot on. There are points in the book which I could relate to my short journey so far, but it also highlighted aspects I had not yet considered and could potentially trip me up in the future. The structure of the book makes it simple to read up on quick, actionable advice, whilst the chapter segmentation is perfect for revisiting, which I will undoubtedly do during any future raise. *The Money Train* is effectively your own investment advisor in a book.'

Tom Jelliffe – Founder, Tzuka

'I know I will come back to this book time and again for reference in the future, and I expect other founders to use it in the same way. *The Money Train* is a great analogy because that's exactly what it feels like.'

Sam Peters – Founder, Octaive

'I've been hugely fortunate to have had David as my mentor and chairman, and in that time his knowledge and guidance have been invaluable with regards to fundraising and investor relations. This book is the next best thing if you're not so fortunate and will provide you with plenty of good actionable advice that you will and should keep going back to.'

Prash Naidu – Founder, Rezonence

'A great idea will never succeed without proper finance. But where to start? *The Money Train* is an expert guide to raising capital. A brilliantly written book by someone who's lived every high and low of building businesses. David knows exactly what he's talking about and after reading his book, so will you.'

David Mansfield – author of *The Monday Revolution*

'I really enjoyed the read. Lots of good advice in there brought to life with useful anecdotes, quotes and real-world examples.'

Hugh Campbell – Partner, GP Bullhound

THE MONEY TRAIN

10 THINGS YOUNG BUSINESSES NEED TO KNOW ABOUT INVESTORS

DAVID PATTISON

First published in Great Britain by Practical Inspiration Publishing, 2021

ISBN   978-1-78860-194-8 (print)
       978-1-78860-193-1 (epub)
       978-1-78860-192-4 (mobi)

Cover credit: Photo by Sawyer Bengtson on Unsplash

Practical Inspiration
Publishing

Contents

Foreword   *ix*

Introduction   1

Part I: Three questions   **5**

Why is there a need for this book?   7
What does the investment market look like?   11
Are you ready to start the investment journey?   27

Part II: The ten things   **31**

1. Is everyone headed in the same direction at the same speed?   33
2. Taking money from the right people   45
3. Investors only care about one thing   61
4. Raising money at the right time at the right price   71
5. Raising money at the wrong time at the wrong price   85
6. Be ready for due diligence   97
7. Cash arriving is the start, not the finish   111
8. Take targets seriously   123
9. A deal's a deal   131
10. Be ready to switch strategies   143
Summary of the ten things young businesses need to know
about investors   151

Part III: Information   **155**

What help and advice do you need, and where do you find it?   157

Abbreviations, information, resources and jargon   *173*

About the author   *183*

Foreword

'We need to accept that we won't always make the right decisions, that we'll screw up royally sometimes – understanding that failure is not the opposite of success, it's part of success.' — Arianna Huffington

In this quote, Ariana captures the reality facing any entrepreneur on their journey through life. Founding a business is easy. Making a success of it is extremely hard and cannot be done without the help and support of many people. And time. And money.

My long, yet exciting, journey with Blue Prism was successful by pretty much any measure. A British software company that became a 15 year, overnight global success story, with a highly successful IPO in 2016 and fabled unicorn status. Starting with two people and a great idea, we were able to execute with the help of many people: directors, employees, customers, business partners and, of course, investors.

The one area that you don't want to be learning from a mistake is in the fundraising arena. In this practical guide to navigating the scary world of corporate finance for entrepreneurs, David Pattison uses personal experience and many anecdotes from extensive real-world research to illustrate the opportunities and potential pitfalls of engaging with different types of investor. From making sure there is alignment around the board table before raising money, finding the right management team and how you can expect investors to react in various circumstances, through to the importance of building trust with your investors by delivering your promises, this is a wealth of advice that I wish had been available to me in our early days.

An essential read for any business founder or early stage CEO.

Alastair Bathgate
Founder, Blue Prism

Introduction

'When things go well, they go really well. There is nothing intrinsically good about owner-managed businesses and nothing intrinsically bad about investors.'

The quote above is from a lawyer. Lawyers see the whole range of investors and investment options and the variety of owner-managed businesses looking for investment.

'Raising money: You don't know what you are getting into. There is only one way to go: Fast growth and losing control. It gives you a five- to ten-year window.'

This second quote is from the founder of a very successful business who has raised money on four occasions.

'People looking for money have no real understanding of the difference between investor types.'

The third quote is from an adviser who works with young businesses.

'Innocence is culpable.'

The final quote is from the same lawyer as the first quote.

In a nutshell, this book is for young businesses that have decided they need to raise money to move forward. It's about preparing yourself for the investment journey.

Once you take investment, all the stakeholders know where that journey ideally ends: A sale that generates a significant profit on everybody's investments – whether those investments are your time, sweat and early funding or from the investors who have put in their money along the way.

That is why this book is called *The Money Train*. Because it is a real journey, and once you decide to take investors' money, the destination is set. You are on a track. It's a real commitment and it can feel like a fast ride.

You will want to be at the front of the train, driving your business to future financial success. If you don't maintain some sort of control, at best it will be a very uncomfortable ride. At worst, you will get derailed.

There have been, and will continue to be, a lot of very successful investment partnerships with owner-managed businesses. The aim of this book is to help your business to be one of those successes.

This book is an enabling book, helping you to prepare for that investment journey. Good preparation is the best time you can spend. If you are looking for cures to an investment mistake, then it is almost certainly too late.

Get the investment process right and you will enjoy all the fruits of a successful relationship and maintain control. Get it wrong in your very first negotiation and the commitments and clauses will be carried over and multiplied every time you go back for more money. There becomes less and less room for manoeuvre and almost no way of fixing it, unless you are very lucky. That is why this is book is an enabler and not a cure.

In putting the book together, I have spoken to business founders, lawyers who spend a lot of time in this space, corporate finance advisers, independent CFOs and investors. I have used a lot of their stories and observations, but no name-attributed quotes.

I have also called on my own personal experiences, gained as a full-time CEO at two companies that had successful multi-million-pound exits. Following on from that, the next stage of my career has been spent helping young businesses start, grow, raise funds, thrive and sell, sometimes as a hired hand, sometimes as an investor/adviser and often as a chair.

The first of my two CEO roles was with a company I founded with two partners, PHD, which is now owned by the American holding company Omnicom and trades in over 80 countries around the world.

The second was with the digital media business iLg. I was hired to sell on behalf of the founders and the various investors. I successfully sold the business for a significant sum of money and a couple of years later, as a non-executive, watched the same company go into liquidation in 40 minutes – 'character-forming', I think they call it. But I learned so much about investors, lawyers, bankers and founders.

More recently, I have taken those learnings and passed them on to a range of companies that I have helped over the years, acting as a 'wingman' to watch their backs. It's never plain-sailing, and you learn more from the hard times than you ever do from when everything is running smoothly.

Setting up your own business is the most exciting, energizing, terrifying, motivating, lonely, emotional and rewarding thing you will ever do. Once you decide to bring other people's money into your business, you have to get it right. That's why I have written it down. If you have decided that you need money, this is how to prepare to get it on the best terms.

PART I

Three questions

Why is there a need for this book?

'You really don't know what you are getting into.'
'I wouldn't change it. The company might not exist.'
'Most stressful experience of all time.'
'Our early investors were amazing.'
'I felt like an incompetent criminal.'
'They promised a lot and delivered little.'
'Their value-add was immeasurable.'
'They didn't really understand our company or our market.'

These are just some of the things that founders of young companies have said to me about the process of getting investors into their businesses and, I think you will agree, they cover a bit of a range. How on earth do you decide who to go with and on what terms? It's really hard and not at all straightforward. You will need luck and timing as well as good advice and a lot of commitment and energy.

For young businesses looking to raise the first round of serious funding, the founders and executives are at their least experienced and most naïve. The first negotiation will be the one that will set the future shape of the business and put in place a whole range of parameters that the next set of investors will use to inform their investment offers.

Getting the first major raise right, at the point at which you have the least experience, is a very difficult thing to achieve, let alone getting it somewhere near perfectly right. And you will almost certainly be negotiating with people who are very experienced at doing deals. You will need to prepare well and take a lot of advice and help. You will also need to take it very seriously.

What do I mean by a first major raise?

A first major raise is likely to be after you have raised the first investment from friends and family to get the business started. I will go into more detail a little later in the book.

Why a book about raising money and dealing with investors?

Over the years I have seen the effect that looking for investment has had on companies and their owners, which one should never underestimate. It's usually massive. I have led teams, been heavily involved or have been a light-touch adviser to companies looking for funds to develop their businesses. I have learned a lot about what to do, and what not to do.

Why now?

There is an ever-increasing amount of investment money available from an ever-increasing number of sources. There are various business models, but one model expects young companies to take on investment and, in many cases, 'enjoy' debt in their business. Through personal experience (some really good and some less so!), I have learned a lot about what to look for and what to avoid.

I want to help companies prepare and ask the right questions of themselves and their potential investors, to prevent them making some of the mistakes I have made and witnessed along the way and to learn from things that helped me succeed.

Fundamentally, I want to help to ensure that the first investment negotiation doesn't become a suffocating straitjacket for the future.

There isn't a specific chapter on how to negotiate. This is by design because there is no single solution. Every negotiation is unique and different. However, I will attempt through the book to identify the things to look out for: What investors really mean when they say certain things/behave in a certain way; how to get the best you can for yourself/other founders, your shareholders and your company; what legal clauses really mean. I will use personal examples as well as experiences from people I have met along the way.

> I want to help to ensure that the first investment negotiation doesn't become a suffocating straitjacket for the future.

Here is the first piece of advice: listen, a lot, to other people who have been there and done it.

I will also use personal examples from another part of my life. At the age of five I wanted to be a racing driver. That ambition stayed with me through my life, to a point where I thought it was too late. However, in recent years I had the opportunity to fulfil that ambition and become a racing driver. I approached it as a project and whilst doing it I learned that there were many applications from the business world that helped me achieve success. I did it for six years and it was amazing – and I did pretty well, as the range of unattractive trophies in my house would attest to. I found that I took some similar approaches to my racing as I have in business and, as a result, I have used racing analogies as examples throughout this book.

Here is the first racing analogy: rather like being on the Money Train, when you are on a racetrack going fast, you don't want to leave the track and you know in advance where the destination is. Being well prepared and in control will get you there intact and enjoying success.

What does the investment market look like?

The investment market is complex and very hard to generalize. There is a lot of money out there waiting for you. It comes in different shapes and sizes and with different degrees of difficulty to get hold of.

Why is there so much money around?

Since the economic crisis in 2008, it has been very hard for people to make money in what were the traditional investment markets. Interest rates have stayed low and equity markets are complex for all but the very well informed. Other global events, such as pandemics, terrorism and wars, continue to make it harder to profit.

So smart people with smart money are trying to make money in other ways. Art, wine, property and classic cars are just some of the areas that money has poured into. Values have skyrocketed and this has of course attracted gullible followers who don't really understand the markets they are getting into – the very people who will almost certainly take the fall when the markets reset themselves. And markets always reset themselves at some point.

One of the other areas money has poured into is the business investment world. Knowledge of the investment world is much more readily available, and governments have introduced attractive tax-saving schemes to encourage investment in young businesses. In the UK this includes the SEIS and EIS. These schemes give individuals and companies instant tax relief, provided that a number of criteria are met.

As a result, the market is much more attractive and accessible for individuals with investment money. In addition, there is a significant variety of new, more formal, investment funds in the market. Again, a lot of them come from followers who don't fully understand the markets or companies they are investing in. But there is a lot of money available, and as time has gone on this money has potentially become more and more available to fledgling business start-ups.

Why do they want to invest in you?

They want to make some money. A lot of money can be made if yours becomes the next well-known success like Apple, Facebook or Amazon, or even a less well-known but successful unicorn business.

What market are they looking at?

Employment market expectations go through cycles, and increasingly the cycle seems to be that anyone leaving education needs to come up with an idea for a business – tech-based, and probably an app. OK, that's a sweeping generalization, but I do think that the pressure now is on coming up with an idea and setting up your own business.

The reason is that technology innovation has opened up a lot of markets within markets. Niches within niches are now accessible and acceptable. Wide-ranging generalist businesses are no longer the norm.

The plan for the aspiring college-leaver entering the employment market in the 1980s, 1990s and early 2000s would have been to enter the worlds of investment banking or strategic consulting with one of the large, established companies. There was a bit of a crossover from the late 1990s and through the 2000s, when it became about working for the big tech giants like Google, Facebook and Amazon.

With the coming of the digital age, the huge reduction in research and development (R&D) costs, the fragmentation of markets and the relative simplicity of building something, there has been a huge rise in optimism amongst new workers. No one needs to build a mainframe today, and the march of cloud-based services has made development more and more accessible and affordable. There is also a lot of investment money around to bring these ideas to life. They just need to look successful and scalable.

As the markets continue to fragment, no idea is too small, and there have been and will continue to be some spectacular successes from this new tech world. That's why investors want to invest in you. There is potentially big money to be made for them and for you.

There is a model for these businesses to succeed and grow. But beware: this model is largely constructed by the investment industry. A clear case of the tail wagging the dog.

So – surprise, surprise – the models that are deemed by the investment community to be the sexiest and most investable are the ones with a lot of investment funding built in. However, this 'one size fits all' model doesn't work for every business, and for some it's a model that is seriously flawed.

Let me explain.

Flawed businesses survive for too long

One of the consequences of an investment market with a lot of money and investors with low levels of market knowledge is that limited ideas and flawed businesses survive for longer than they should.

What does a flawed business look like?

At a business's early stage, it's very easy to spot a gap in the market. It is much harder to see if there is a real market in the gap. It's also relatively easy to find someone to fall in love with an idea and put funding into it. Anything in the tech area is particularly easy to entice people into.

> It's very easy to spot a gap in the market. It is much harder to see if there is a real market in the gap.

As an example, I see loads of ideas that rely on advertising revenue as the main income generator. Quite apart from the fact that it's really hard to bring advertisers' attention to your offering, there isn't enough advertising in the world to make all of these businesses profitable. But early money gives false hope. A second round makes you feel invincible, even if the business isn't really performing. As one founder said to me: 'You believe everyone will see the proposition and the money will keep coming.'

In my experience, founders often kid themselves for a long time about this. They are always the last to see their business is flawed. If sales aren't going well, then for them it is the market that doesn't understand. There is nothing wrong with their offering.

The reality check is usually harsh and comes when a round of fundraising doesn't work because the potential investors can see that the market really *does* understand. And the current investors have run out of money or commitment. It's brutal when that happens, and I have witnessed founders being emotionally crushed by this.

Eventually it's the false hope that kills you. But the reality is that it's the investors that have allowed the business to survive for longer than it should have. The shape of the investment market has driven the business, not the market that the business operates in. It probably showed some weaknesses, but the signs have been ignored by the over-excited early investors and the equally over-excited founders.

And then, in a heartbeat, the investors stop investing and it all comes crashing down. It's very painful, and the investors run for the hills with as much of their investment as they can and claim their tax reliefs and capital losses. The business founders have no confidence left, are financially spent and, at best, have a very unclear future.

The exceptions

As always, there are some exceptions which make it hard to know whether you are a flawed business or are just needing some luck or are having timing issues. Some businesses can take time to catch. They can be slightly ahead of their time, get the first marketing iteration wrong or have the wrong people leading them.

I worked with one company that took four years to start really flying. In those four years it nearly ran out of money on three occasions. There was always a gap in the market and, over time, a market appeared in the gap. The proposition was changed, and the company grew on a double-digit monthly basis. It had always been the right idea and, in reality, it was the real trading market, not the investment market, that reshaped the offering.

Ask yourself the hard questions

Why is all this important? Because when you are working out whether you need to raise money, and how much, be honest with yourself. Ask the following questions.

- Is there a real market here?
- Where is sustainable revenue coming from?
- Where is the competition for that revenue?
- Have I got a real business?
- Do I just need more time?

Just because the market model is investment-driven doesn't mean that everyone will succeed. Investment driving accelerated growth isn't the only answer. The 'go big or go home' mentality isn't always the best route. Sometimes doing that old-fashioned thing of reassuring yourself that the business can make a profit without investment is a good starting point.

One of the businesses I was involved in from the start only took money from the three founders, including me. Despite lots of offers on the way through – and, to be honest, a few close scrapes with cash flow – when the time came to sell it was a simple process and the terms were what the founders wanted, not what the outside investors wanted. Could we have grown more quickly with outside investment? Almost certainly. But at what cost? The founders also achieved their goals of securing both a good financial deal and a future career with the purchasers.

It's the simplest business model to retain control in, and all of the success is yours.

Where do you start in the investment cycle?

By understanding your business financially. The first thing to do is to work out if you need any money at all. If you can see a way of building a business without needing to raise any money, or by raising a smaller amount, then look very hard at those options. For a number of businesses, if a model can't be put together that works without investment, then there probably isn't much of a business. If such a model puts the business's growth back by a number of years, then it probably needs investment. If it's a number of months, then it might be worth reconsidering.

One founder I spoke to said that one of their big regrets was not having a grip on their financial model early enough. If they were doing it again, they would have looked at a model that did not require any investment, just to see what that looked like, to help them decide whether investment made a big difference. It undoubtedly would have been lower-level and slower to build, as well as personally more painful, but it would have given them more control for much longer.

I pushed them on whether they would have done it differently and not gone down the investment route, and they said they wouldn't have changed a thing. They simply wished they had known what the alternative was, and in addition they felt it would have been much better business practice.

Part of the reason they didn't know was because they had inadequate financial management experience in the business. I will make this point again and again through the book. It never fails to amaze me how slow new businesses are to get good financial planning advice into the company. It is always seen as an unnecessary cost. It isn't unnecessary. It's an investment that will pay for itself in ten minutes. I see it every single time. Even if you have to hire an outside resource in the early days, then do it.

> It never fails to amaze me how slow new businesses are to get good financial planning advice into the company.

There are lots of businesses for which 'no investment' isn't an option, so you need to work out if yours is one of these businesses. Good examples of exceptions include businesses that require heavy R&D investment or manufacturing plant, or businesses that need to grow quickly and run very fast to take advantage of a market trend: 'bubble businesses'.

Who are the potential investors?

On the face of it, the investor market looks easy to understand and well ordered. The truth is that there are a lot of nuances within the structure. A seemingly unlikely investor can always make an exception because they really like your business: 'we don't normally invest at this level/in these markets, but we want to go with you'. Likewise, a potentially perfect investor really might not like your business: 'it's too early/too late/the wrong market/the wrong price'.

As an aside, the unlikely investor is usually just that, and if they aren't used to working with a business like yours then I would question whether they are the right partner.

On a simplistic level, investors in the market fall into two sectors: the *emotionals* and the *rationals*. Understanding the crossover point is really important in both the way you deal with those investors and what they expect from you.

The emotionals

The emotionals are easy to understand but the hardest to classify. In a nutshell, an emotional investor is almost always an individual investor. They come in a variety of forms, with seed investors, angel investors and high-net-worth individuals being the most regular. Some angel investor networks are brought together into one fund by investment companies whose investment is usually made up of individuals putting in identified amounts in their names. It's their own personal money and that's what makes it an emotional decision. Being seen to pick a winning business is part of their motivation.

There is one thing that unites almost all emotionals: tax relief. There are a number of very well thought-through government-funded tax schemes that allow investors to reclaim some of their investment and, if it all goes wrong, they can then claim some or all of the losses against other gains and income (see 'Abbreviations, information, resources and jargon' at the end of the book). In their eyes, the major thing that you have to do is to ensure that the company maintains its tax relief status.

At the very early stage, investment usually comes from people you know. They are generally described as seed investors. Either you and your partners know them or, as one corporate financier described them, they are 'friends, family and fools'.

The demands of seed investors are not usually very onerous and as well as tax relief, all they really want to do is back someone they know, for you to remain in business long enough to return their money plus a bit at some stage in the future. They will normally agree to the slightly over-optimistic valuation you have set. The shareholders' agreement (if there is one) is usually pretty simple and because you know everyone it is relatively easy to manage this group. They usually leave you to get on with it and are not really very demanding. If it's the 'bank of family and friends', then its potentially even less demanding but probably even more emotional.

Angel investors and high-net-worths are pretty much the same thing. Tax relief is again a big driver for these investors. They are normally people you don't know, but could be friends of friends or acquaintances. These investors are sometimes bought together by an angel network or non-institutional fund. They will want properly lawyered paperwork and will be more demanding than seed investors.

They may well demonstrate a bit of bravado to prove what good negotiators they are. If you find yourself in a room full of them, as often happens with the networks or funds, it can be excruciating to watch them try and out-ego each other. As a lawyer said to me, 'the worst investors are the high-net-worth funds that have no discipline'.

However, if you find the right ones, they will be your most loyal supporters and your best 'foul weather' friends and will invest again, sometimes when others shy away.

The rationals

The rational investors are broadly the institutions. These are the venture capital investors, the private equity investors and a relatively new group called *growth capital* investors.

They are rational because they are driven by the demands of the investor clients in their funds. These are almost always institutions, although there can sometimes be very wealthy individuals involved. The rational investors have targets by which they are measured and systems and processes that they adhere to.

It's very difficult to generalize who does what in the rational world, and this isn't helped by the general media, which takes little interest in differentiating or paying attention to the detail. So, there are always blurred lines and exceptions.

Broadly, venture capital is interested if a business is successful in generating revenue at a sub-£10-million level but is not yet profitable. Such an investor would look to make five to ten times its money in five to seven years. It would take more risk than private equity, hence the word *venture*.

Private equity is interested when a business is making over £1 million of EBITDA (profit) and would look to get three times its money in three to five years. There is a slight variation that sits largely in the private equity space, known as family funds. These are exactly that – funded usually by one family, as a result they tend to work to slightly longer timelines. As an aside, I have always found them well organized and professional to deal with.

Growth capital sits somewhere in the middle, for businesses that are not making a profit, but are growing at about 30% a year and probably need about £10 million+ of investment.

As I said, these are generalizations and there are other options that can offer investment. A venture capital trust works broadly on the lines of venture capital but the investors in the fund are taking advantage of enhanced tax breaks. They also tend to have longer timelines as the funds don't usually have fixed exit dates. However, you do have to be sure that all of the criteria to keep the venture capital trust tax-efficient are kept in place at all times. It can be the case that if your business loses its tax status then the whole fund, not just the investment in your business, loses its tax status. And that is a very expensive mistake, not just financially for the fund, but reputationally as well. So, expect added scrutiny.

Where else does money come from?

Corporates

A lot of the big traditional corporates have venture arms that invest in early start-ups. By this, I mean the huge, globally well-known corporate giants. They are definitely on the rational spectrum. Their investment can look very tempting. The initial reaction is often that they will provide 'a customer base we can sell to', or 'market knowledge for free', or 'a leg up'.

However, if you come to sell and they have a significant share, or they make up a large part of your client base, then you can paint yourself into a corner, with the only viable purchaser being the initial corporate investor. Not many competitors will want their main rival sitting around their boardroom table. It doesn't really lead to a competitive process and the price paid will reflect that.

The media have made investment from the corporates look very attractive, with headlines such as 'XXXX Tech Company Pays $1 Billion for a Start-Up that Doesn't Make a Profit'. It happens, but it's very rare. Some corporates have such investment funds so that they can look cutting-edge and cool. However, not surprisingly, they can be very corporate and rarely have staff that understand the pressures of starting and running a young business – mainly because they haven't done so.

As one finance consultant said to me, 'If a corporate is interested, go and look at the venture capital market. I would take a 20% discount on valuation every day from a venture capital fund versus a corporate.'

If it's a fund from a known entrepreneurial business, like the new tech giants, it is likely to have a different attitude, but probably with the same level of scrutiny and desire for control.

Trade investors

Trade investors don't really invest in this market as they are rarely able to compete on valuation and tend not to want to take massive risks or large shareholdings. They are more likely to get involved early or be the purchaser at the end of the cycle. When they are investors, they tend to tolerate under-performance better.

Funding from trade investors is very unpredictable money, here in the good times and gone in the bad, which is not good if you are looking for a second investment in the future. As one corporate finance adviser put it, 'They have very short memories, so in long bull market runs they become active and then shut down when their share price collapses in bear markets.'

Accelerators

There is a slight hybrid which is early-stage and quite institutional, and that is the category of the accelerators. They tend to put relatively small amounts into very young businesses and offer facilities and resources to these new companies. These facilities are normally paid for by the investment they make, as well as charging you a monthly fee. So, if you are not careful, you can end up paying back all the money for the services provided and being part-owned by an accelerator – a painful truth that many don't realize until it's too late. There is also no guarantee that the next round of funding will arrive. However, accelerators are usually linked to a lot of angels and high-net-worths and will do their best to introduce the next round of investors.

Accelerators work on the premise that a few will succeed, thus paying for the ones that don't, at the same time as charging everyone for everything on the way through. It's a good business model for them but can quickly be overwhelming for you.

Crowdfunding

The final investment route I want to cover is crowdfunding. This splits into two types: reward or equity crowdfunding. Sometimes it can be both of these.

What most people think of as crowdfunding is specifically *reward* crowdfunding. This can be a very useful way of raising funds if your product or service is a thing that people can identify with and want to be part of. An investor puts in money and gets the product or service at a favourable rate. Sometimes that is the offer, and sometimes there is some equity attached.

Equity crowdfunding is just that; the investor buys equity in a similar way to the standard investment routes, albeit usually at a lower funding level.

I haven't had much experience of crowdfunding and there are some well-established fundraisers that can organize the whole process for you. It can be quite time-consuming and not every business achieves its funding goal. It normally helps if your product is recognizable to a wide audience.

There are two things to watch out for here. First, one founder told me that that by the time he had raised money through a crowdfunding site, he had been charged close to 10% of the money in fees. Second, an institutional investor warned me that having crowdfunders as existing shareholders can lead to complications later down the line, just because of the sheer number of shareholders.

But there are some successful examples from this route. It means you are unlikely to have a dominant investor, which should leave you to get on with it. Communication is vital and you have to beware the disaffected investor who has put in a relatively small amount of money but can make a lot of negative noise on social platforms.

Other funders

There are regional, government-backed funds that are driven by different criteria. I know of one fund that only looks to break even on its investments, but its success is measured by the number of jobs it creates in a region. There are many other regionally focused funds that are about stimulating growth in their areas.

Ethical funds and social impact funds are also on the increase, whether they be focused on gender, ethnic, environmental or ethical lines. The millennial generation is much more likely to care about where the fund is investing. They may even seek out funds that specialize in just these areas. The more general funds are definitely starting to be affected by these relatively new market entrants.

An investor I know lost a deal to an ethical fund even though the deal was less good for the founders. As the investor said, 'The young aren't kidding when they say it's not just about the money'.

Part of the decision for the founders looking for investment will be the company the funds keep in the shape of their other investments. This is a trend that I believe will only become more significant.

Occasionally, the really big players – typically hedge funds – become enamoured with the early-stage, young business sector. They invest, often make mistakes and then pull their support overnight. They call it being decisive. My advice would be to give these investors a very wide berth.

One thing to know. One of the reasons for the growth in specialist funds (e.g., ethical/gender/ethnic) is that traditionally the investment sector is a very male-dominated and aggressive sector.

> The investment sector is a very male-dominated and aggressive sector.

Investors are, in the main, competitive and macho. Like the rest of the world, this is being forced to change, but very slowly. When dealing with them, be yourself; you don't have to change, but be prepared for this when you come into the market. It can be intimidating, uncomfortable and overwhelming if you aren't ready for it.

And finally, there is a lot of jargon in the investment world. I have tried not to use abbreviations and shortcuts in this book, but have attempted to explain some of the language in the section 'Abbreviations, information, resources and jargon' at the end of the book.

That's a quick dance through the main areas of the investment market. You will have noticed that there are a lot of options if you have decided you need to find some money. And there are 1,000 more nuances that I haven't covered.

The investment ladder

As you will read often in this book, there are many 'norms' in the investment processes but no real 'norms' in the fundraising hierarchy. What does that mean? It means that *how* investors invest and behave will always be true to type, whether it be emotionally or rationally. However, *where* they invest can be a moveable feast. Within the hierarchy, investors can always make an exception and invest (or not) outside of what would be their investment criteria 'norms'. So, money can present itself from the least expected sources or won't come from where you expect it to.

The progression for fundraising would typically be: raise some very early money to establish the idea (often called bootstrap funds); raise some seed capital to get it going; get some top-up money to get to proof of concept and some revenue and then raise big funds to accelerate the business by volume/geography/product lines and more; then a really big raise to max out the company potential. These stages would typically be called *bootstrap funds, seed capital, interim top-up, series 'A'* and *series 'B'*.

To prove the point that nothing is linear, the step across from emotional to logical can happen in the top-up or series 'A', but not exclusively in either.

THE INVESTMENT LADDER

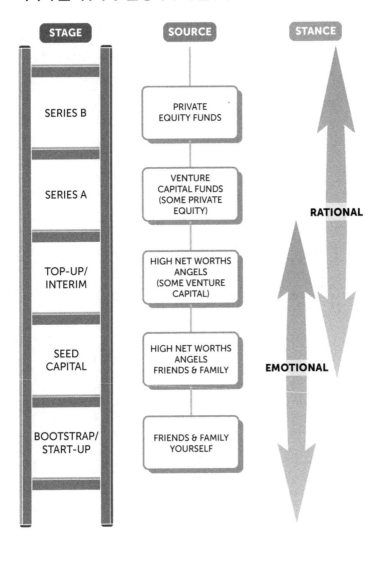

STAGE	SOURCE	STANCE
SERIES B	PRIVATE EQUITY FUNDS	
SERIES A	VENTURE CAPITAL FUNDS (SOME PRIVATE EQUITY)	RATIONAL
TOP-UP/ INTERIM	HIGH NET WORTHS ANGELS (SOME VENTURE CAPITAL)	
SEED CAPITAL	HIGH NET WORTHS ANGELS FRIENDS & FAMILY	EMOTIONAL
BOOTSTRAP/ START-UP	FRIENDS & FAMILY YOURSELF	

Are you ready to start the investment journey?

The key question is: 'Do I need to raise investment money?' As discussed in the last chapter, the market will almost certainly expect you to raise some money and will encourage you to do it. What will the investment ladder journey really look and feel like?

There are many routes your investment journey could take but I suspect it might end up looking a bit like the following.

- You have had your idea. It's a risk to go on your own. You decide to take some early investment to slightly lessen the risk.
- You have some success, not profit, but you generate some revenue and you have 'proof of concept'. You are feeling optimistic but underfunded.
- The idea works. People get to hear about it. Potential investors get to hear about it. You feel popular and have investment options.
- You are 'hot'. Just think how you could accelerate this success with more resources, more people... and, of course, more money.
- You take the money; you spend the money. Profitability is two years away and the cash runs out in 15 months. Then you take some more money and have to promise more accelerated growth.

And so, it goes on – the Money Train at full speed and in all its glory. It will all feel very fast. It will seem like every investment conversation you have moves the goalposts in terms of what you need to achieve to get that investment. If you aren't careful, your business will be shaped by an investment market influence, not necessarily by the strengths of your people and your offering.

How to decide if you need to take investment

Before you get onto the investment ladder or climb aboard the Money Train, there are a lot of questions that need answers. Some are as follows.

- What would funding add to the business?
- How much do I need?
- How much time would it save?
- What would be the costs of raising money and diluting shareholding and controls?
- What multiple of success would it add?
- What would happen if I didn't raise money?
- When would I need the money?

And the following, which is not to be underestimated: what do I have to offer investors?

- Are there tax breaks I can offer to investors?
- Does my time frame look attractive?
- How much might an investor make?

The biggest change resulting from taking investment is that the business is no longer 100% your baby. And if, having taken investment, you are seen to be behaving as though it still is, then you will hit problems pretty quickly.

The assumption for this book is that you are now at the point where you are starting the fundraising journey. You need money. You broadly understand the structure of the investment market.

The rest of the book is a guide to what to ask, what to expect and how to approach the processes. It's for the young businesses looking to raise some money, mainly covering the range from start-up and seed investing through to series 'A' with venture capital funds or venture capital trusts. It will also cover that switch from the emotional investor to the rational investor – the step where, time after time, I see the relationship between founders and investors under the most strain.

PART II
The ten things

1

Is everyone headed in the same direction at the same speed?

Here we go with the first motor racing analogy. When I was being taught to drive fast by Joe, my coach, the first thing he told me was that I had to lift my head and look at least one or two corners ahead. This makes sure that you don't spend all your time looking down, to be surprised when you look up by how quickly the next obstacle is coming at you. It makes for a smooth drive and a faster time. It's very easy to say and very hard to do. You are effectively planning where you are going rather than focusing on where you are now. In racing, looking at where you are going is really important to future success.

It's just as important in business to do the same thing. The difference is that in racing it's a physical thing, whilst in business it's a mental thing.

But why is this important for understanding what investors want? Because when they are looking to invest, they will not only want to know that you are planning for the future, but will want to be reassured that the management team is aligned and committed to that future. In addition, they will want you aligned with them once they have invested.

Where do you start?

You have had your great idea. You have your team together, or sometimes you just have yourself. Everybody in the business is very energized and, although trying unsuccessfully to hide it, apprehensive. You have toasted your future success but haven't yet mentally spent the money that you hope to make. Or, more likely, you are looking at the mountain in front of you and wondering how on earth you are going to get to the top.

As an example of how big that mountain can look, when we won our first client at PHD, our total first year's fee was one third of what I had personally earned in the 12 months prior to us starting the company. There were three of us. To get to earning what the three of us had previously been earning would need us to have nine clients of that size. And there was a lot of other stuff to pay for as well. To be honest, I couldn't see where all these clients and all this revenue would come from. But with a personal need to succeed, a commitment to my business partners, a pregnant wife, two kids and a mortgage to finance, it certainly meant it wouldn't be for the want of trying. I had no choice; that mountain had to be climbed.

Everybody outside the business will be wishing you well and privately thinking that you are mad, unable to see why you would put everything at risk.

Setting up your own business is a huge commitment. If it was easy, then everyone would do it. As discussed earlier, with modern technology and niche businesses in abundance, on the face of it, it looks easier than perhaps it was in the past.

It's going to be an amazing success. Of course it is. If you don't believe that going in, then you shouldn't do it. Everybody wants success. But there are real dangers in assuming that everybody wants the same success and that they want to achieve it in the same way.

Spending time working out what everybody wants at the beginning of the key phases is time very well spent. Of course, you can change your mind as time goes along. You don't know what you don't know, and things will present themselves that are impossible to plan for. But there are some things that you can do to try and get the shareholders pointing in broadly the same direction. This needs to be revisited on a regular basis and at various stages of the company's development. It will help to cut any tension between shareholders and, much more importantly, find out where the often costly differences lie.

> You don't know what you don't know.

What people want needs to be well understood and most often it's agreeing time frames that are probably the key to finding the solution. There are three key stages at which this needs to happen. The first is when the company sets up, when the shareholders are usually the founders and occasionally a helpful early investor. The second is when a new shareholder becomes part of the company. This can be a senior hire/internal promotion, which is usually pretty easy to deal with, or an investor looking to come into the business, which will bring a whole lot more complexity. The third is once a significant/influential investor is on board and is part of the business moving forward.

Stage one

Let's look at the first stage. When you start and the idea is formed, it really is worth looking everyone in the eye and asking the following questions.

- Are we doing this as a good cause or to fulfil an ambition?
- Do we want to change the world?
- Is this a lifestyle business with modest targets?
- Do we want to pass this on to our kids?
- How long do we want to do this for? What's the time frame?
- Is this just about money and, if so, how much is enough?
- What financial needs will we have on the way through?
- What pressure will we get from partners/family?
- If we sell, do we want to stay in the business? If so, for how long?
- Could we work for someone again?

As I said earlier, revisiting these questions on a regular basis is important. When I was at PHD, I was one of three founders. We would find time on a couple of occasions a year to get away from the business and discuss the big opportunities and challenges that were in front of us. The first thing we always did was to play 'stick or twist'. This was basically the three of us saying out loud whether we wanted to keep going ('stick') or look to sell/exit ('twist'). As a three, we always came up with the same answer. We had all set up the business for the same reasons. The fact we always agreed was very helpful for us as individuals and great for the company. When we chose to 'twist', it was unanimous and driven by market forces that we had all spotted.

In my experience, initially, most young companies have fairly modest ambitions. Usually, the founders want to make some money, want people to want what they are selling, want to be part of a great team and want an exit in around five years. As one adviser said, 'The modesty of ambition is always a surprise'. As an aside, it's never five years. It's almost always a minimum of seven.

There are exceptions to the modesty of ambition, but these are usually people who, on the face of it, don't lack confidence in their own ability. However, in truth, they are hiding behind bravado and an adrenalin-driven need to succeed. There are some very confident founders out there and they can be successful, but I have often found that it is a lack of self-confidence that drives founders' success – always running hard and fast to stay ahead of whatever they view as the next problem to solve.

When it comes to 'how much is enough?', most people want to make enough money to sort out the debt in their lives and get the family through the school years with a bit left over at the end. Having said that, almost without exception, if there is a sniff of success in the business this number goes rapidly north as time goes on. And the less confident catch up with their more confident peer group pretty quickly.

Getting the early legal agreements to line up with the shareholders' ambitions is also very important. I don't intend to go into much detail about what a shareholders' agreement is or does (although I guess it's fairly self-explanatory!) or how articles of association work, other than saying that the shareholders' agreement usually protects the shareholders and the articles of association protect the company. The articles are normally overridden by the shareholders' agreement, but I have seen it the other way around.

What these documents do is to lay out how the company and its shareholders can behave, the buying and selling of shares, board construct, governance issues etc. Again, these need to be agreed and thorough, without being a straitjacket on the business and how the executive operates. At the early stage it is often the case that the articles can cover the eventualities of that time, and there is no need for a separate shareholders' agreement.

Getting the right advice at this time from the right lawyer is so important. The very best lawyer you can afford is a must for the whole of your journey. If you are going to spend time and money on one adviser, getting a good lawyer would be number one on my list. Look on it as an investment, and not a cost.

As an example of how not to do it, when we set up PHD we used a lawyer who was a friend of a friend. Their skill base was in the rag trade; we were in advertising. Therefore, our lawyer had no knowledge of our sector. We also had a trade investor as a fourth shareholder, and we had to put protections in for this shareholder without giving away the company. But we spent all of our time writing agreements that were about failure – about what would happen if we went bust. Nowhere in the documents was there anything to cover success. So, when we did enjoy future success, there was no mechanism to get back shareholding and nothing to compel the trade investor to sell to us. This inevitably led to some friction at a later date. This friction could have been avoided by using the right adviser, who would have advised us to plan for success as well. I guess having a bit more confidence in our potential success would also have helped. From then on, I have always made the best lawyer a priority, whether it be for my personal business or for the companies I work with.

> The very best lawyer you can afford is a must for the whole of your journey.

It seems that we at PHD were not alone in committing our mistake. As one investor and adviser said to me, 'People don't plan for success'. Make sure you plan for success!

Stage two

At stage two, you are much further down the line. New shareholders are introduced either as new members of the senior team through hiring or promotion, or as investors.

> People behave badly when money is at stake.

Protecting the company when giving shares to employees, no matter how senior, is relatively straightforward. There are a few attractive HMRC-approved share schemes that allow you to award minority shares to employees and new hires. The UK has an EMI (Enterprise Management Incentive) option scheme that is very tax-efficient. These schemes usually have very flexible rules that can be put in place to help you protect the company. Amongst other things, they can cover:

- the price of the shares
- when they are awarded and when they vest
- how they can be sold and at what price
- what happens if an employee leaves
- the definition of a good leaver and a bad leaver
- whether the shares have voting rights
- whether a dividend is paid if the company is profitable

Never fall into the trap of trusting that people will behave properly. People behave badly when money is at stake – particularly when they are non-founders. They can often take the rather perverse stance of placing a lot less value on shares than you do, whilst assuming a right to own shares and being unrealistic about what a meaningful shareholding is.

Things can go horribly wrong if you don't protect the company. I know of a company in the finance sector that gave a minority, but significant, shareholding to one of its senior staff, who was actually a relative of one of the founders. The company trusted that as a family member and senior employee, this person was going to stay for the long term and decided not to put in place a particularly tough shareholders' agreement. Two years later, this person resigned, got full value for their shares and then set up a competitive business funded by the money from the share sale. Ouch!

As one adviser pointed out, 'You get what you structure; make sure that you understand the implications of the share structure you use'. If you are worried about upsetting the team member, then don't be. You are protecting the company. It's not personal, just good governance.

You should always remember that your most precious asset is the equity in the company. It will be the thing that potential buyers will pay a multiple on at some point in the future. Don't give it away. This can be a very easy thing to do early on, when you have no money.

There seems to be more awareness of shareholding in the employment market now, and sharing equity with senior employees is generally the right thing to do. But make sure that the company is protected and that you don't end up with your shareholding scattered all over the place with a number of ex-employees. I have seen companies be too generous and others be too frugal. It's really hard to get right, but in my experience most founders are too generous early on when they have little money to pay with, and that makes it harder to be generous later on. Giving *sweat* equity is fine, but make sure people sweat for it first. As an example, giving early equity to an adviser with a good black book of contacts looks very attractive, but that black book runs out pretty quickly. What are you then left with, apart from someone else owning a bit of your company?

When more formal investors get involved it is often a turning point for the company. The original seed investor shareholders get diluted and there is then someone, or something, else that has ambitions for the business and ambitions for whoever they represent. It is really important that the founding shareholders share the same view of the future of the company and the time frames that everybody is working to. There is nothing more off-putting for an investor, particularly an institutional investor, than a team with different plans. Before you meet them, agree what the plan is and stick with it through all the conversations.

That doesn't mean you should misrepresent the truth. It means you should come up with a coherent plan. If there are exits involved, then show how these will work and how they will be funded (or not). Retained equity (allowing leavers to keep their shares) could be an answer. Whatever happens, you have to be joined up, or the investor will take advantage of your weakness. It is, after all, a negotiation – and they want the best terms they can get.

Stage three

The third stage is slightly different to stage two and occurs after the investors have become part of the company.

Let's look at funds first. They will have targets that are not directly related to the individual businesses in which they have invested, but they have to keep their clients happy, so their portfolio needs to hit its targets. These targets will usually revolve around timing and returns, i.e., how long they want to stay invested for and how much money they want to make.

These time frames have to be stuck to, driven by their investors who want their money and profits returned at the time they have been promised to them. Most funds have a life span of about ten years. Early investors in the fund probably have a time frame of around five to seven years, but late investors may well be looking to exit within three to five years. That sounds like a long time, but if you are growing fast, you then have two problems on your hands.

- You won't want to sell the company and the amount of money needed to exit the investor will have gone up significantly as well.
- Raising money from new investors to exit an old investor can be notoriously difficult.

There are a few things you can do at this stage.

- Be clear on what it is that they want and when they want it, and plan for it. One thing is for sure: it won't go away.
- Make sure that the timeframe is set by the decision-maker at the fund, not just your board fund representative.
- Keep asking the question on timing and don't assume it will always be the same answer. Be ready for a change. Like you, they don't know what they don't know.

As an example, my very first non-executive role had a board that contained six investment companies. Yep, they raised a lot of money, many times! I was the only board member who wasn't an institutional investor. We spent the whole of the board meeting arguing about valuation and ignoring the fact that we missed the revenue target every month. Within the investor group was an early investor who had been with the business for seven years and wanted to exit, and a new investor who was invested for the long term and wanted to get the business moving and growing. There was a lot of tension around the table. The executive was in a no-win position and because of the company performance there was no appetite from either the current investors or new investors to buy the early investors out. The board meetings were just a waste of time and energy. Not once did we focus on yet another missed revenue target. There was no forward planning or helpful advice.

This went on for years. It was no surprise that the valuation went up consistently, but the company performance remained an unchanged struggle. These shareholders were never going to be aligned and the company made no plans to get through this. It wasted so much time.

Once the focus eventually moved on to the right metric of the company performance, the CEO and CFO were the eventual casualties. But it was really the investor shareholders that were at fault.

More difficult to predict are the high-net-worths, who will almost certainly be some of your earlier investors. I will talk in later chapters about their behaviours and inputs, but understanding what they want from investments is often complex and sometimes not logical. In almost all cases it is a unique set of reasons and no two individuals are the same.

In the main, the individuals want to take advantage of some advantageous tax break, often before the tax year finishes. In the UK, the EIS (Enterprise Investment Scheme) and SEIS (Seed Enterprise Investment Scheme) are two very tax-efficient schemes. But they can also be drawn in because they like what they see (either the product or the people, or both) or a big potential upside. As one corporate finance consultant told me, they can be 'wealthy privates who have too much money and don't care, or can be completely the opposite'.

Understanding what they want and how they will measure you in their eyes is vital. These individuals can be very distracting – they are often well-meaning, but distracting and time-consuming nonetheless.

Getting in line

Whoever is investing in the business will almost certainly insist that the management wants the same thing. Or, if they don't, the investor will want to know why and how that will be managed. Being surprised six months in is not what they want and will immediately start the downward spiral of mistrust.

What is almost impossible to achieve is to find another investor to simply take out an existing shareholder, particularly at full price. There is always the 'Why?' question, and no matter how good the answer, it's never good enough. So, it usually falls to the company to try and solve this, often leading to having to take on serious, long-term debt that then acts as a drag on the business and distracts everyone. It will also tie up a lot of money in legal fees. Do whatever you can to avoid this. Early, good advice and well thought-through legal documentation that allows for early exits for founders/shareholders will really help. These are rarely at full value, so they discourage shareholders from selling and make it easier to sell at a discounted price.

It is also possible for early investors to be bought out as part of later rounds of investment and even for founders to take some liquidity (sell some of their shares), but only as part of a bigger raise. An investment to take out one shareholder at full price is very rare.

One other thing that can cause a problem in future fundraising is an over-complicated shareholding structure. If it is over-complicated, it could give shareholders different rights and make it very difficult for the shareholders to have an aligned view on the future, as different share classes could be rewarded in different ways at different times.

One company I worked with had seven different types of share classes in place before it had achieved its first million of revenue. All of the classes had different rights and different rewards. This caused all sorts of issues in the fundraising processes and often resulted in yet another class of shares being added. Eventually, everyone saw sense and the share structure was completely changed, but not without – you've guessed it – much distracting negotiating time and a lot of expensive legal fees.

Having said all of that, as mentioned earlier, there are always things that you don't know you don't know. Things come up – illnesses, founder fall-outs, poor hires – and people change. There will be things that you can't plan for. Its then that you need a clear head and the support of all the other shareholders to get through to the other side in control, solvent and with as little distraction and angst as possible.

Good legal advice in the early stages of the business, and well-constructed shareholders' agreements, will go a long way to helping get through the unexpected.

All aboard the Money Train: Is everyone headed in the same direction at the same speed?

- Ask all your fellow founders the difficult questions on what they want and when.

- Have an aligned management view on the future when encouraging investors.

- Get the business set up legally to manage as many future eventualities as it can.

- Protect the company when issuing new shares to new management/shareholders.

- Make sure all of the new investors and the current investors are aligned on the future.

- If differences arise, plan for them (as much as you can).

- Get the best lawyer you can. It's an investment, not a cost.

- Have an uncomplicated share structure.

2

Taking money from the right people

When I was choosing the people I wanted to race with, it was really important that I chose well. It's a stressful environment. In the racing world there is little time for niceties, and you have to communicate quickly and directly. The wrong partners would have introduced constant friction and stress and ultimately led to under-performance or, worse, a literal car crash.

I drove in a 'pro/am' series, and I was the 'am'. Whilst I wanted someone who shared the same values, I worked out that I needed my pro driver to be completely different to me. I needed a teacher, someone with experience, knowledge, a different thinker, the ability to get the best out of me and a firm but friendly face. Joe turned out to be exactly that and he was the one who would make me a better driver. Precisely because he was a pro driver.

Looking through the other end of the telescope, what did Joe want from me? He wanted to be paid, a fast and reliable car to be able to show his skills and to get some results. He realized that challenging me fitted with my personality and making me a better, faster driver made him look good. He understood 'the am market'. As a result, whilst racing with me, he got noticed by a big manufacturer team and subsequent to driving with me he became a factory-funded driver. We both got what we wanted from the relationship.

Conversely, Rob, the team engineer, and Chris, who ran the team, needed to understand me. We needed to communicate a lot more about just about everything. They needed to be a bit more like me –

more empathetic and coaxing, rather than challenging. They were the supports to the product, and that product was me! You can probably see where I am going with this regarding choosing your investors. You need the right people in the right places. If you have the choice, you need to choose well.

The early-stage investors

Most new businesses do actually see themselves starting with a baseline business model. It just starts in a different place, as it assumes some very early seed funding. It is done by taking seed investment from 'friends, family and fools' ('the three Fs'). They add what is widely called sweat equity and free advice, and there is your baseline – instantly forgetting that the seed investment is actual investment.

Seed investors and sweat equity

Seed investors are very often the people who get your business started. They are usually family members, friends or friends of friends. *Sweat equity* is a term to describe the work, knowledge and skills that are put into the company for no money. Founders very often refer to sweat equity as their contribution to the company. This is often because they don't have much cash to put into the company, and are not keen to take out massive loans. Sweat equity is also used to reward early advisers and contributors. It's a tool widely used by new businesses and founders, who often undervalue this equity and give it away to the outsiders too freely, storing up issues for the future.

The seed investor raise is always interesting to observe. It can actually be a daunting prospect, as many founders have no idea where to start. Almost always, the founders underestimate how much they need and are often embarrassed to ask for what feels like a lot of money but in the business world is a small or modest amount. As one adviser observed, '90% of founders are utterly clueless at this stage and the other 10% know less than they think they do'.

The good thing at this early stage is that, whilst you may have no real knowledge, you are usually dealing with a very friendly investor group. You almost certainly know them well, and if you don't, they are probably interested because they either love you or what you do.

At the seed investment stage, you need to ask yourself the following questions.

- How much money do I really need to get this off the ground?
- Am I going to take the money as a loan or sell some of the business?
- If it's a loan, do I guarantee it?
- If I sell some of the business, what valuation do I use?
- Can I help these investors by offering a tax incentive as part of their investment?
- Where can I get help with this?
- What legal help do I need to get onboard?

Don't be shy in asking for the right amount of money. It will give you confidence and save you from asking for more in the short term. I have seen founders struggle to ask for £5,000 because it feels like a lot of money. It isn't. This is backed up by an adviser who told me, 'The founders thought £5,000 was a lot of money and were delighted to get it. They needed £50,000 but didn't have the confidence to ask for it.'

Whatever you raise, make sure you value this money. Use it sparingly. Remember: this is the period when the business will either show some promise or reveal itself to be unworkable.

Go to family and friends first. They may invest or they may point you to people who will. And then try and find some 'fools'. It's the wrong word really, but there are people, like me, who are happy to take a risk on a very early investment – not because they always work (they often don't), but when they do, they work really well, not just financially but also in terms of helping the business achieve success. These people are usually friends of friends or people with an industry reputation that are known as early investors.

Having said that it, it can feel like the most daunting of fundraisers, because it's the first. It is extraordinary how quickly founders then move on from the seed investors, rather dismissive of the role they have played.

It is very easy to see your seed investor as a means to an end, but it is worth treating them with respect early on. Through the investment cycles they will usually get diluted down to virtually nothing. But beware of them using an old voting right to hold things up in the future, and you might want them to put their hands in their pocket again. Don't be dismissive of the seed investors. Without them, you wouldn't have started. They can be the best investors that you ever have. They tend to be very supportive, not too demanding and will sign up to a high valuation at an early stage. If you are very lucky, they may also be the people who will fund your second round. They may be the only investors who will willingly help to fund early cash flow issues. I have seen some hugely supportive investors in the early stages.

Another benefit is that if things start to go well, they will quite often introduce their wealthy friends at the subsequent funding stages as well.

There are a few things you have to beware of at this stage. Don't take money from the person who can't really afford to lose it. If it's their total savings and in their head they see this as a route to millions, they will be distracting, continually checking up and constantly fretting. This will put strain on your workload and if it's a personal relationship it will create an emotional strain – sometimes irretrievably. Ask them the following questions before they invest.

- Can you afford to lose this money?
- What are your expectations?
- How do we ensure that our personal relationship doesn't suffer?

Another thing to ask is whether they are looking for a job. Sometimes the individual investors will use their funds to try and buy some work. They will offer to do all sorts of things for you. It is easy to believe that they just want to help, when in fact they don't have enough to do. Maybe they are coming to the end of their full-time working career and want some meaningful employment. These people often come with outdated ideas, fragile egos and a rather over-inflated opinion of their worth. They will happily try and impose old-fashioned practices on fresh new businesses, insisting that they are the ones who drive and run these practices. This is sometimes very hard to resist if they are family members, but you need to work out what they are really bringing. Beware.

On the other hand, the very best early seed investors will sit in the background and offer help when they are asked. They are people with relevant market knowledge and an up-to-date and useful black book who will help to set the company strategy and can make contacts or add value to the company when looking to sell or raise further funds.

The right people can add significant reputational and therefore financial value to a business. The company you keep says a lot about you.

Which brings me to sweat equity, which is equity given to people for a contribution that doesn't include money. It's widely used by founders who can't afford to pay for early advice/help. I have seen it used time and again, and in the early stages of a business the founders are usually over-generous and don't value their own equity. A few percentage points here and there soon add up. This is often allied with poor legal documentation, which makes it impossible to get back. Buying someone's experience for a one-off project may look attractive, but when it's done what are you left with? Some equity gone and someone with nothing to add. Trust me: you will resent this person pretty quickly. If you are going to offer something, then make sure you are in control of it. Share options instead of shares, for example, with clauses that limit the upside.

And unless you are really sure, do not offer a board position to anyone who asks for one. The board needs to be a decision-making body, not a badge of achievement worn by non-inputters.

Non-financial trade investors

It's not strictly money, but there is an option to get another type of shareholder on board. You can look to take help from other companies in the sector. This usually involves things like office space, financial reporting help and access to a range of other resources. Sometimes it includes money. However, this is another area that young businesses over-value and where they can get themselves tied up and into tough spots.

Offers of help from someone in the sector can look very attractive: no-risk office space and good-quality financial help from day one. What's not to like? There might even be some money involved. How do you pay for this? Usually with equity. And usually with a lot of equity because you are so grateful.

Two examples here. First, when we set up PHD, in order to de-risk a little we took some money and support from another trade player. We were grateful and because we were new to everything, we were unsure of our chance of success. We were encouraged to value this trade help at 25% of the company. After 18 months of success it was clear we needed nothing from the other company. Sure, we would not have launched without them, but we had given away a quarter of our business with no way of getting it back. We should have negotiated more cleverly or found someone to do it for us.

The second case concerns a tech business that set up and gave away 50% of its equity for office space, some promised business and not a lot else. The deal also came with all the legal paperwork having been produced by the trade 'help'. I think you can see what's coming. After a very successful launch and continued growth, none of which was down to the promised business from the trade help, the founders wanted to get back some equity but that was only available at a ridiculous price hidden somewhere in the legals. So, the only way of doing it was to put the business into liquidation, which they did and started again, costing a lot of blood, sweat, tears and money. What a waste. Less generosity and more attention to the legals would have solved all of this.

Please be very careful in giving away generous amounts of shareholding for what looks like a lot of great resources. It might even be the thing that gives you the confidence to start the business – like when we started PHD. But if you have anything that looks like success, you won't need that help for very long. If you give equity for this resource, make sure it's not too much and that you can get it back at a reasonable price.

In truth, at the seed/sweat equity/trade help stage, you aren't really on the Money Train. You are probably waiting at the station for it to arrive. You have taken money but it's almost certainly friendly money. In the eyes of most young businesses, the investment conversations actually take place at the round of funding after the seed capital. From the second round on it tends to be people you don't know. Uncharted waters. The Money Train is now ready for boarding.

Working out what you need

For most, the requirement for further funding usually revolves around growth and new developments, speeding up the pace of growth of the business and identifying specific areas that need to be built into the business but aren't currently covered. The two things are usually linked, as the faster growth will be delivered by the areas the money is wanted for. Technical development or manufacturing plant can also come with heavy cash requirements.

Before you go looking for money, try to answer the following questions.

- How much money do I need?
- How quickly do I need the money?
- How long will that last me for?
- How much of the company am I prepared to sell?
- Do I want an active investor or an arm's-length investor?
- Is there any experience or knowledge that I need to add to the company?
- How many investors am I looking for?
- How likely am I to need follow-on investment, and how much?

Once you have the answers to these questions you will usually be in a much better place to understand the type of investor you want. If the answer is 'I don't know' or 'I am not sure', then focus on coming up with an answer by researching or resetting strategy. Come up with an answer that is sellable and works.

> Investors are not attracted by just being the funder of cash flow or keeping companies afloat.

The best position for you to be in is to have some choices. The more you understand about what you want/need, the clearer it will become and the more attractive you will look to the investment community – or at least to the right type of investors. It may also weed out some of the inappropriate investors.

It's worth giving a health warning at this point: investors are not attracted by just being the funder of cash flow or keeping companies afloat. If you find yourself in this situation then expect it to cost you a lot of equity and ultimately a lot of money. More of this later in the book.

The individual investors

You are probably now at the stage where you are looking for money from unknown sources. Depending on the level required, these could be individuals (angels/high-net-worths) or some of the smaller funds. In the later rounds it will almost certainly be investment funds, as individuals tend to only invest to a certain level. In my experience it's very unlikely that you will get an individual to invest more than a low six-figure sum for a single investment. But on occasion I have seen larger amounts.

Once you know what you need the money for, and how much, then you start looking for the right individual investors. That is really hard; there are lots of them, but there aren't many obvious places to go and find them. And if you do find them, they are very hard to research and check up on – particularly the individual emotional investors.

The angels/high-net-worths are definitely the most difficult to gauge. They can be the best investors and the worst. One founder said to me that if he could have done all of his fundraising with high-net-worths, he would have. He described them as 'very good in the dips', 'ready to go again' and 'don't always need all of the facts'. Conversely, a corporate financier said that high-net-worths were 'always the most problematic and almost impossible to do due diligence on'. So, working out which camp they sit in is really important.

Getting the money is the most important part of the process. But never underestimate the importance of what you want the investor to be doing once they are part of the company, or the influence they may feel they are owed. They may want a big hand in either the strategy or even the day-to-day running of the business.

What you really want are investors you trust, and who trust you, who will let you get on with the running and growing of the company, only becoming involved when invited in. If you bring them in to offer advice in one or more areas, then let them know what it is that you want and encourage their input. This, of course, is the perfect world. The reality is that even with the individuals, the bigger the investment, the more involvement they want. This is understandable, I would say.

Communicating regularly with the individual investor is really important. A business I know made a seat available on the board to represent all of the seed/angel/high-net-worth investors, representing about ten investors in total. I always thought this was a good idea. It cut down the amount of time that the CEO needed to spend keeping everyone up to date and made the group feel important and listened to. You could also offer a board observer role. This does exactly what it says; there are no voting rights and the observer is not a company director but has the right to attend board meetings and observe. One word of warning on this role, though: in my experience they seldom just observe and very quickly behave like a full board member.

I have learned over time how to behave as an investor. When I first started in advisory roles, I know I was far too eager to please and offered to do anything and everything. I soon learned that what companies want, and need, is wisdom and experience they can act on. As one founder said to me, they want 'a voice of reason offering the occasional hand on the shoulder either yanking me back or giving me a pat'.

Founders want to do it themselves, not have unpaid investors do it for them. In the worst cases, they probably felt slightly threatened. I have now learned that the best route is to be asked and invited, rather than to impose.

Where I have found there to be exceptions is if the adviser has a paid input role, such as chair (sometimes unpaid in the early stages) or mentor.

Through experience they can sometimes see something coming that the founders/company have had no experience of. Examples include:

- cash flow issues
- recessions
- bad debt
- disfunctional management teams
- poor financial systems
- an unclear proposition
- client dissatisfaction

The bottom line would be that if you are paying an adviser/chair you should assume that you want to hear what they have to say. Otherwise, you should probably stop paying them or replace them.

If they aren't in an input role then my advice would be to lay out prior to investment what you expect, or ask the investor to tell you how they want to be involved. Write it down and agree it. By the way, you don't have to agree to all of their demands, particularly if they are only going to end up with a small minority equity share.

Don't be embarrassed to do your due diligence on an individual. Ask for references. Talk to other CEOs of companies that have worked with these people.

One final thing: we talked earlier about the tax benefits available to individuals and to some investment funds. For individuals, this is often the key driver to making the investment and they don't really care too much about what you do with the money once you have it. This is amazing but true. Getting this type of investor is a good thing. If you deliver them a tax-free profit at the end, they will love you forever. The angel networks are a good place to go to find this type of money.

What about the funds?

In theory this is a little more straightforward. There are a range of questions to ask the funds to help you work out if they are the right partners. Some of these are appropriate to the individual investors, but as I have said, it is much harder to generalize about them.

Some of the questions I would ask include the following.

- Why are you investing in us?
- What time frame are you investing across?
- Will you follow on if needed?
- What return are you looking for?
- Where does this investment sit in the life of the fund?
- What controls do you typically ask for?
- Can you show that you have the funds?

There are more, but these are the factual questions I would get to quickly. The initial stages are all very exciting for everyone, including the fund representative. But the rational investors will come quickly, and you don't want to be wasting a lot of time in a honeymoon period that is going nowhere. Find out why they want you, find out what their expectations are, find out if there is a time frame and find out if they really have the money. And if they are proposing phased payments then make sure they have all of it available when they say they will. The funding may come with performance requirements from you, but that isn't unusual.

I have seen good and bad examples at this stage. In one case I saw good and bad all in one negotiation. Having been encouraged, an early investor in a MarTech company I knew was approached for the next round of funding. In relative terms it wasn't a massive amount of money. The investment was needed to invest in people and tech to get the company through to the next big fundraise. At every board meeting and in every conversation the signals were positive, and a few months before the money was needed the investment process started.

What should have been straightforward seemed to take a long time. Getting the money secured was always 'a week away' (by the way, it's always a week away, like the cab that is always five minutes away). At the eleventh hour and fifty-ninth minute, the investment committee got involved and turned down the request on some spurious basis. The committee was made up of people who didn't know the business or understand the market, and bizarrely were not prepared to listen to their own representative. It was one of the most excruciating meetings I have ever been in.

It turned out that we were the victim of some internal politics driven by a merger of two funds and we were, unknowingly, in the wrong camp. Our fund representative was so embarrassed by the behaviour that they resigned.

With no back-up, the company had no plan B and a very bleak (cash flow) outlook. From almost nowhere came a white knight in the shape of a direct competitor to the original investor. Having been a victim of politics, we were now profiting from them. This had been a company that we had stayed in touch with through the process. Another very good practice.

No one is very sure whether it was the business that drew the investment or the chance to put one over on the other investor. It didn't matter; in either case the company then had a future. But the initial assumption and the signals suggested that money would be there from the original investor. Instead, the company should have secured an agreement after the first investment, committing them to putting in the extra money when required, or not. This may have come with a list of key performance indicators (KPIs) that needed to have been achieved but it would have been clear. Clarity, clarity, clarity.

In another example, in a series A round, a FinTech company I knew had the luxury of choice. It chose, on paper, the easiest money. It turned out that the money 'promised' after the first payment didn't really exist. Some months after the first investment, this caused all sorts of strife and the business had to take a completely different course.

> **Don't be intimidated by a fund.**

Don't be intimidated by a fund. Make sure they are the right people for you. Check them out as much as they check you out – both the fund and the individuals, particularly your day-to-day representative. Talk to other companies that they have invested in. You will find that people are really happy to help, really happy to share experiences, both good and bad. There is almost a pride in battle scars. Remember that the institutions will feel that they 'own' you, no matter how much of the company they have. Don't let them act that way, unless they do own you.

> The institutions will feel that they 'own' you, no matter how much of the company they have.

Remember, some of these investment relationships can last longer than a marriage. You don't have to love them, but you do need to respect them. Take the time to get to know the individuals.

They need to show understanding of the market that you are in and what it is that you are offering in that sector. Get to know the person who is going to be your point of contact. Get them to show you an example of what they can do for you before they invest.

> Some of these investment relationships can last longer than a marriage.

None of this should wait until after the investing; it's too late by then. Try and hang onto the right to an independent chair for as long as possible. This can be an invaluable role if there are differences between investors and the company.

Once you get to big private equity investments, they will usually want to either appoint their own chair or at least have a big say in who it is. In most of the raises before the private equity raise, investors will want a chair that can work with the company executive. The independent chair can often act as a buffer between the executive and the investors. Their role is defined as making sure that the company acts in the best interests of all the shareholders. A good independent chair can also significantly reduce the friction around a boardroom table.

If it's a fund that works with tax breaks, a venture capital trust or an EIS fund, for example, then their job is to maintain the tax break through the life of the investment. So, the investment phase will come with the same (if not more) rigour that any other fund would use prior to investing. They will also monitor very closely the journey through investment life. They have to make sure that your company is tax-compliant for the life of the investment. It is probably the number-one thing to achieve for you and your fellow founders. Be really clear on what this compliance means in reality to the company and its day-to-day operations.

Understanding what any investor brings or wants is fundamental to successful founder–investor relations. There is a lot you can do to find these things out. It needs a little confidence and the right questions to be answered. They will ask a lot of you, so don't be afraid to ask of them.

Working with investors who have either run or started a young business is really helpful. It helps with understanding the issues. As a founder said to me, 'Investors who have been there are disproportionately important'. Sadly, amongst institutional investors they are very rare to find.

A few other things

> If there is money there to be taken, then take it.

Having said all of the above, one of the things that was unanimous amongst founders and advisers who had been in the fundraising process a few times was that if there is money there to be taken, then take it, even if you aren't looking for it. Don't take it at any cost, but take good money on good terms, the rationale being that you never know what's coming and timing is never perfect. You never know when an outside event might put huge pressure on your cash flow. Taking it whilst it's there can help you get through the unknown and/or drive the strategy harder and faster. But remember: it needs to be good money on good terms.

I have talked a lot about understanding how investors can help, but make sure you deal with realities. All funds will tell you that they can bring a lot to the table. As one freelance CFO who has seen a lot of deals said to me, 'Don't be taken in by promises of input and value-add. It's almost always promised and rarely delivered.' My personal experience would have me agreeing with this, but I have seen it on very rare occasions be transformational.

I heard one funny story from a corporate finance adviser. He knew of a fund that had forgotten about an investment. It was the last investment to be harvested in their fund. The fund hadn't heard anything from the

> VCs will make a decision on where they invest, and an individual will make a decision on whether they will invest.

company but knew that it had been through a number of structural and name changes, resulting in a severe dilution of shareholder equity. The assumption was that their less-than-1% shareholding was close to worthless. The fund fixed up a meeting and left it with a big smile on their face. Through a mix of being the perfect benign investor and some incompetence, their investment had grown by tenfold and had transformed the overall performance of the fund. In hindsight it was genius!

Finally, remember the key difference between individual investors and institutional investors. A CFO said to me, 'Remember that VCs will make a decision on where they invest, and an individual will make a decision on whether they will invest'. Institutions have to invest their funds; individuals don't. This can lead to timing issues, more of which later in the book.

All aboard the Money Train: Taking money from the right people

- Don't take seed investors for granted. Treat them well.

- Don't be over-generous in giving your equity away for external sweat equity or trade help, and make sure you can get it back if you need to.

- Work out what you want investment for. Ask yourself the right questions and have good answers.

- Understand what the individual investor wants from their investment.

- Do due diligence on the funds and individuals that are looking to invest. Ask lots of questions and look for proof of successful previous investments.

- Be clear on what you want from any investor (and agree it).

- Do not be intimidated by the funds or their 'we own you' attitude.

- Take good money at a good price when it is there.

- Remember that institutions need/have to invest; individuals don't.

3

Investors only care about one thing

Racing drivers are very selfish. They only care about one thing and will do pretty much anything to achieve it. They want to win, and they want to beat everybody on the grid. It's why the most mild-mannered person can turn into a different animal as soon as they take their seat in the car.

I can remember sitting on the starting grid with only one thing in my mind: how to get in front of the people in front of me, and how to make sure those behind me didn't get past. The warm-up lap before the start was the moment the selfish side of me had taken over.

My pro driver Joe sometimes shocked me with his desire to win. In normal life he could be reasonable, charitable and helpful. When he was in a racing car, he was unreasonable, uncharitable and unhelpful, unless it helped him/us win. I get that now, and it is why he is as good as he is.

The same is true of investors in your business, particularly the rational institutional investors. They only care about one thing: their money. They want to win and to beat everybody else in the market.

Why rational investors only care about their money

If there is only one thing you take from this book, it should be this: investors only care about their money. They will all claim to be different but, with one or two nuanced exceptions, they are not.

This is because they are all measured in the same way. To understand this, you need to understand how these funds are structured and how everybody involved is measured.

> If there is only one thing you take from this book, it should be this: investors only care about their money.

Seed investors/angels/high-net-worths are almost always individual investors. This makes these relationships easier to gauge and manage. In most cases they still only worry about their money, but they may well have already received a significant tax break, which can take a slight edge off their expectations. Alternatively, they might be someone you know or who loves what you do. However, deep, deep down, they do care about their money. They are just a little less bare-faced about it.

Venture capital and private equity funds are just that; what everybody forgets is that these funds need to be funded. They are funded by individuals and by institutions. An investment is not the fund's own money, and the funders might be entities such as other investment funds or pension funds. This is the reason that the investment funds are more rational, because they have the equivalent of clients who expect investments to be made diligently and profitably.

The bottom line for the funds, therefore, is that the only real measure of their success is how much money is actually being made by their investments – the returns to their client investors.

As discussed earlier, most funds have a life of around ten years. Most of a fund's investments are made in the first three to five years of its life. The rest of the time in the fund is spent harvesting the money from the sales of the investments. This latter stage is also the time when most funds will be looking to raise the money for their next new investment fund. So, they will want to have some successful harvesting going on to prove to potential investors that they can make money for them next time around.

How do the funds make money? It's almost always the case that they are funded by the 2-and-20 formula. The fund earns 2% of the invested money as a management fee on an annual basis and then takes 20% of the upside when the businesses it has invested in sell, or the fund divests itself of a shareholding. All of the fund's income is driven by financial performance, which is why it only cares about its money.

The fund may have to wait seven to ten years for the 20% upside, but in the meantime it will be reporting back regularly to its investors on your company's progress. Through the life of the fund it will want to be able to show that the value of the fund is increasing. It will want to show how clever it is at investing and what good deals it has done. It will be continually checking on the valuation of your business so it can show the value of its deal base. This is also used as a very important marketing tool for when the fund is trying to raise the money for its next investment. Again, it is all entirely money-based, which is all a fund cares about.

The growth in the number of funds has increased the competition in the market for attracting investors into funds. This, in turn, puts pressure on fund performance and therefore the performance of you – and, more importantly, your business. It's rational and it's linear.

It might not feel fair when things are not going to plan for you, but it's totally predictable and you should know this from the outset. It's why you should never expect a fund to care about anything other than how to get its money back or make more money from whatever the trying circumstances are. It won't give you a break. You have signed up to an agreement, with performance criteria, and if you aren't meeting those criteria then all bets are off and a re-negotiation is coming your way. This re-negotiation will only benefit one side of the deal: the fund investor.

Even a massive worldwide event outside of your control will attract little sympathy from the investor. As I said, rational and linear – and that's how you have to deal with them.

I know of a digital marketing business that had been sold to a private equity purchaser just before the world economic crisis of 2008 hit. To be honest, the company didn't stand a chance and was hit very hard through the crisis, as were most businesses. It tried to right itself over the next 18 months but was weighed down by the debt that had been injected into the business by the investors. Whilst it carried a lot of debt, the nature of the market it was in meant that it acted as an agent and therefore at certain times of the month had a huge amount of cash sitting in its bank. When it lost a large client through no fault of its own, its investors and funding bank could see their money disappearing quickly. They therefore waited for the company's bank account to contain maximum funds and then shut the business down. It closed in 40 minutes, leaving 110 people without jobs and owing a lot of people a lot of money. It was brutal, but the investing fund had its money back, as had the bank.

There are lots of lessons here, but in particular the absolute confirmation that looking after their money is the centre of the investor's focus.

Don't expect empathy

What does this mean to the companies that they have invested in? It means that they should not expect very much leeway once a deal is done, and any re-negotiation will only go one way: a worse deal for the company and its executives than the one that is already in place.

It also means that the prospect of receiving some emotional understanding is never on the table; this is not the way the funds are structured and not the way that the funds behave. Everything is black and white. There are no shades of grey.

With that, you could make an assumption that all fund investors are sharp. Some of them are, but most of them are looking for good companies to put good money into. Destroying value in the company they have invested in is clearly not the plan.

But it can be so easily done. Barriers go up; the initial warmth of the first meeting can soon turn to ice and distance; mistrust grows and the relationship becomes like a bad marriage. Most of the time this happens without the investor even realizing it. To the investor this is a transaction and nothing more. To the founders it is a whole lot more than that.

> Founders of businesses only really suffer high highs and low lows.

I genuinely feel for founders at the lack of empathy shown by potential rational investors. Every founder I have spoken to has said the same thing, and it really bothers them: there is no recognition. Founders of businesses only really suffer high highs and low lows. As one founder said, 'they just didn't get that I have a lifestyle of highs and lows and nothing in between'. Another said, 'investors need to understand the highs and lows of a start-up business. It's a rollercoaster and it needs empathy.'

There is no in-between. Founders do genuinely lie awake at night worrying about all sizes of issues and problems. The logical investors very rarely even acknowledge this, demonstrating that they really don't understand. They should – but please don't expect it and don't let a lack of emotional understanding cause friction and distance.

In Chapter 2, we noted how one founder wished that all their investors were high-net-worths. In their eyes, the emotional investors were more empathetic and therefore easier to manage. I think what they were really saying was that they found them a whole lot easier to bend to their will. The institutional investors are definitely not for bending.

There are some very smart institutional investors who *do* get it. Unfortunately, they tend to be the ones who take advantage of your emotional ups and downs during the negotiations.

One of the ways of avoiding disappointment over the lack of empathy is to recognise that the more you can negotiate in the initial agreement, the greater the likelihood that you have covered most of the eventualities that

> Hire the very best lawyer you can afford, and if you can't afford the best early on then change when you can afford to.

will come your way. You won't be able to aim off for everything, and you don't want to stray into the world of the ridiculous.

But, if nothing else, make sure that there is no ambiguity in the agreement. 'Open to interpretation' are not the three words you want to hear from your lawyer if you are two years into a deal and there is a problem to solve.

Again, the requirement for a good lawyer is a point worth making. Hire the very best lawyer you can afford, and if you can't afford the best early on then change when you can afford to. In this arena, loyalty to 'the friend' who helped you set up is misplaced. If the advice is wrong, inexperienced or uninformed, they probably won't be your friend for very long and it will cost you.

Investors aren't really different

Let's return to the investors. They all say they are different, don't they? How do you deal with investors who claim to be different?

This is pretty simple: ask them to prove it. What is it that they do differently? Ask for some examples of where their involvement has made a difference, and 99 times out of 100 you will see that there is very little difference. There might be flexibility in time frames or their willingness to follow on into the next fundraiser, but they are largely all the same. They need to perform and deliver financial returns. It's pretty much all they are measured on. That's why their focus is entirely on one thing.

It is easy once you understand this, and a little easier when you work out how to relate and work with it. Difficult times will still be difficult, but an understanding of the other side will at least help with positioning and conversation tone.

I am aware that this book jumps around from the emotional investor to the logical investor. That's because it's very hard to draw a line between the two. It is very likely that in one of your fundraising rounds you might be negotiating with both types of investors. Crossing that threshold is, attitudinally, one of the most difficult parts of the investment process. Again, your first negotiation with a rational investor will almost certainly occur when you are least experienced in dealing with that type of investor.

Do individual investors care more?

Does that mean that the individual investor is more sympathetic? Do emotional investors 'care'? My belief is that they care as much about their money as institutions do. Unless you are born into it or are a lottery winner, making significant personal money is hard and letting it go easily is not what most of these individuals have signed up for.

It is rare for one individual to invest enough money to own a significant minority/majority of a company post-investment. It does happen, but the norm would be for a few investors to take a stake between them. They may or may not know each other – although they tend to get to know each other quickly during testing times. They will huddle together for warmth to try and build some strength, consolidating their shareholding clout and approaching the company as one body.

In the previous chapter I talked about what individual investors can bring in terms of skills, reputation or introductions. They can be easier to manage, particularly in the early stages post-investment. They will be more forgiving and prepared to 'see how things go'. However, when things get tight, they can be the worst investors. At the first sign of a real problem they can run around with their hair on fire. In their eyes significant problems are always the fault of management, not a bad investment decision. *They cannot possibly have made an error of judgement! These are successful people who know how to make good judgements.* However, they can lash out and make short-term decisions that have huge long-term impacts.

I know of a business in the AdTech space that started to run out of money. The most recent investor was an institution which was unable, or unwilling, to come up with the funding that had been promised. The company therefore looked to the earlier individual investors for funding. Instead of looking at the situation rationally and constructively, these investors' knee-jerk reaction was to throw rocks at the management. This was entirely because they were worried about their money and/or being diluted down to nothing with no chance of getting their money back.

None of them wanted to put their hands in their pockets; all of them expected a fairy godmother to arrive, which of course was never going to happen. They turned on the management, ending up with a nearly-bust business and a demotivated team. It wasn't just one investor but a group of six or seven, leading to a mob mentality when calm was needed. Most of the management left over the next few months and a potentially great business that needed some cash is now limping along with broken investor relations.

> You have to deal with the ups and downs of the individual investors' emotions at the point when they don't care about yours.

So, yes, the individual investors also only care about one thing: their money. But whereas an institution is rational and relatively easy to predict, the emotional individuals are just that. You have to deal with the ups and downs of the individual investors' emotions at the point when they don't care about yours.

You need to understand your investors and communicate regularly

With the individuals it is helpful if you can maintain a good personal relationship. Keep them informed. Agree to provide regular updates. 'No surprises' is a theme we will come back to on a number of occasions and something you will read about in most management books.

It doesn't matter what type of person you are or where your moral compass sits; this will make no difference to the way that your investors relate to you. Understanding the pressure the investors are under from the other end of the process is the best advice I can give you when it comes to dealing with them. It's something that has taken me a while to get my head around, and now that I have, I find it much clearer when dealing with current investors or to pitch to potential investors – not easier, but clearer.

A good independent chair should be able to help you navigate through these choppy waters. It is the chair's job to represent the best interests of all of the shareholders. Whilst it is vital that there is a good relationship between the chair and the CEO, it doesn't mean that they should take the CEO's side on every occasion. A good chair will act as a buffer between the interested parties and should be able to take the heat out of most situations – unless, of course, some of the shareholders take against the chair, which brings a whole new set of issues.

There is one other thing to remember. Do not underestimate a change of the investor representative on the board. To the new representative, your company will almost certainly now be on their to-do list. They weren't involved in your deal but will now have inherited whatever place the company is in. They will want to be seen as having made a difference. As one institutional investor said to me, 'they may not have the championing effect' when representing you within their own organisation. They almost certainly will not be fighting your corner as hard as the original deal-maker.

This is a pretty bruising chapter. I have deliberately taken the coldest view because in my experience that is the reality. Sometimes it takes a little while for true colours to be shown. But the bottom line is this: investors of all types only really care about their money and the money you are going to make for them. Get over it. It's the reality.

All aboard the Money Train: Investors only care about their money

- Remember that all investors only care about one thing: their money.

- Do not expect sympathy or empathy from investors. You will be expected to perform and deal with events outside your control.

- Try and get used to looking at the relationship from the investors' side, without taking their side.

- Put good legal structures in place. Cover as many eventualities as is practicable.

- Avoid ambiguity in legal documents.

- Communicate regularly and clearly.

- Do not surprise your investors. It's expensive!

4

Raising money at the right time at the right price

When you are racing you don't just turn up on the day and hope everything will be OK. Not even the very best can turn up on the day with no preparation and expect to win. There is a whole level of preparation, set-up and testing that has to happen before you get into the car to race. More time is spent on doing all of this than is ever spent racing. The better prepared you are, the more likely you are to succeed. I spent a lot of time (and money) testing and getting the car right and it was the key to me getting more competitive. It also made sure that I gave myself the best chance for my head to be in the right place.

The same is true of fundraising. You aren't going to go into the market and instantly get what you want/need, unless you are very lucky. It takes time and preparation.

If rule number one is that the investors only care about their money, then rule number two is that it always takes a lot longer than anyone says to raise money. Most of that is because it just *does*, and some of it is because delays become part of the negotiation.

If rule number one is that the investors only care about their money, then rule number two is that it always takes a lot longer than anyone says to raise money.

When to start looking

According to my experience, particularly with institutional investors, you should plan on money arriving between nine months and one year from the point that you start to look for it – and nine months would be a good result. Why is this?

As outlined earlier, there are two types of investors: individuals and institutional investors. They behave differently through the process, but both of them start in the same place. They really like what you do and really want to get involved. They have some investment funds and they want to spend them. Remember the nuance that the individual doesn't have to spend the money, but the fund does have to spend the fund.

You have had the meeting with the individual or the representative of the fund and you are 'right in my/our sweet spot', 'perfect for me/us' and investing will be a 'formality'. Except that it rarely is.

I have even seen this become a problem for a current investor who is following on with a second or third investment. They should know the business inside-out, and, to be fair, the representative or individual usually does. But behind every 'I/we really want to do this' is an individual who gets cold feet or an institutional representative who has an investment committee to convince.

What this means is that your fundraising window should be a minimum of 12 months, which also means that you are probably going to start the process of a new round of funding just as you finish the last raise.

This is hugely distracting for the leaders of the business, whose time is best spent on selling services/products and generating revenue. Every founder and every adviser of young businesses I have spoken to has said the same: all investors underestimate or ignore the level of distraction that fundraising brings, and the businesses that are being invested in often make the same mistake themselves. Never underestimate how distracting fundraising is.

> Never underestimate how distracting fundraising is.

There will be times when you hit emergencies and need to raise short-term funds. Quite often, this is a time to go to your current shareholders. You might already know their answer if you asked them the right questions when you took their initial investment, such as the following.

- Have you ever made follow-on investments in the past?
- If we need a top-up round before our next major raise, could you support this?

However, in the main, the best advice is never to be in a negotiating position when the money is quickly running out, and never allow an investor to delay so that they can re-negotiate terms. It's horrible, putting you in the worst position possible. Set timetables and stick to them. Don't be afraid to threaten to walk away. As the 'Wolf of Wall Street' said: 'ABC: always be closing' (which is probably the only advice to take from that film).

When you are leading a business in the fundraising cycles, then the best time to look for funds is when you don't desperately need them. The CEO should be out in the market on a continuous basis. There is nothing more attractive than a business that doesn't want or need an investor right now. It provides the opportunity for you to be relaxed and focus on selling the strengths of the business without a big ask at the end. Individual investors and institutions are constantly looking for options and if they like what they see then they will usually be prepared to wait for you.

But don't waste people's time. A cup of tea is never just a cup of tea. Work out what you want from the meeting and what you are really asking for without asking for it. The investor knows why you are there and so do you. You are selling the strengths of the company and setting up the path to future investment. Make it clear what the future is going to look like for the company and what the plans are. Talk about how you are going to achieve it and how much you might need and when. Don't feel that you can't change things when you next meet. Markets change. People change. Shit happens.

You will get a sense of levels of interest. People will stay in touch. Or, at the very worst, if no one shows interest in what you have to say, you have the time to change the positioning and work hard on making the business more attractive.

One MarTech business I worked with had to change its product definition four times before it became an attractive investment. Not surprisingly, when it became attractive to investors it also started to enjoy considerable success in its market.

You should be in permanent sell-mode. You will have to 'kiss a lot of frogs' during this stage, but you will be in a much better position to know where to go and how much they might be able to invest. It's a really good use of time, even if when it's happening it can feel like a waste of time, and bit dispiriting if you have a run of meetings with not much interest, or if the fund you are talking to is clearly the wrong one for you and you are the wrong investment for them.

Sometimes, if you are enjoying anything like some success and/or you have had a successful raise, then other funds will come and find you. There is more money out there than there are really good investment opportunities. Many of the funds have sales teams looking for the next great option.

I would always advocate going and finding the investors yourself, but sometimes a cold call from a sales team in a fund will take away a lot of the pain.

Actual fundraising

When you are really looking for money, the next thing to do is to try and weed out the time-wasters. This is harder to do with individuals. There is always a level of machismo around this stuff. Something as simple as not having discussed it with their partner might be the real reason for an individual not investing, and most find it hard to own up to this and will keep you hanging on. Try to call them out. Give short deadlines. Get to 'money commitment points' for the investor early. These points are not necessarily the investment, but maybe to committing to the investor's lawyers' fees, due diligence costs or specialist adviser fees. This usually gets some sort of reaction even if it's a further delay, which is often a big clue.

With institutions it is usually easier to weed out the stragglers. This is because if they are really interested then they will start committing to spending money pretty quickly. They know that if they don't do the deal, they will have a bill that will come out of the investment fund management pot, not the invested funds. It also will look like a failure to their investors.

The key is to get a signed term sheet as early as possible. A term sheet is a document that outlines the main mutually agreed terms of the deal. It is short on legalese and usually runs to three to five pages.

Up until agreeing to progress with one offer, this is still a competitive process. Don't get bullied into only getting one agreed term sheet. You should be aiming to get as many as your company resources can cope with. In reality this will probably be two or three. No funds really commit to spending money until the term sheet is agreed and signed. So, the task is to get there quickly and be happy with the terms.

One thing you must achieve early on is to try and keep more than one investor in the process. There is nothing like competitive tension for getting things done.

> There is nothing like competitive tension for getting things done.

You will almost certainly have to commit to exclusivity to one of the investors at some stage, but leave this as late as you can. Exclusivity is a period of time when the investor can do their investigations into your company and put together the legal documents around the investment. Try and make the exclusivity period short. Two to three months is a good target.

What often happens is that exclusivity is granted and then allowed to run on beyond the agreed time frame. There is an assumption that the deal will be done. Sometimes it isn't, or the time drags on to the point where raising money elsewhere looks like desperation, or the people you are dealing with see it as an opportunity to chip the deal. Do whatever you can to stop this happening. Stick to the time frame; they will be committed to costs, and they want an outcome. Put pressure on, and go back into the market if you need to.

Don't think this just applies to new investors. A company I was involved with was looking to raise a round of money. A current investor expressed interest, describing it as 'picking off the low-hanging fruit' in their fund, and a 'no-brainer' to complete in three months. They even came back and offered three times the money that the company was looking for, effectively covering the next round of funding as well. Understandably, the company didn't go and look for money from other sources. Twelve months later, the deal still wasn't done and the business had to completely change its strategy and definitely had a delayed growth phase. Some competition would undoubtedly have helped to speed that along. As an aside, it also tested the trust levels between the company and the investor, which made board meetings and day-to-day communication tense and less productive – never a good look.

It's the same with getting the individual investor to commit their money. If they know there are others interested then they feel more comfortable going with it. Unfortunately, they usually want to be the second investor to commit. Getting the first one over the line is the hardest. But if there are a lot of individuals interested, then, as in most walks of life, the 'thousand flies can't be wrong' maxim seems to give comfort and open people's wallets.

If you get a signed term sheet from an institution or a letter of intent from an individual, then you are some way down the track. We have talked about a term sheet; a letter of intent is a similar instrument, but it is usually sent by the company to the individual investor. This is where there is a major difference in the process. The institutional funds usually drive the terms, but for individuals it is usually you that drives the terms. There is still due diligence to go through, but there is a level of commitment. However, it's worth looking at who is committed to what.

For the individuals, again this process is relatively straightforward. Having come so far, either they will or they won't. It's their commitment and their money, so the decision is generally a binary one which, once made, is made.

For institutions, it's different. You have full commitment but not from the whole organization. The people you have met and have been very convincing with are totally committed to you, the business and the funding. But they have to now sell that internally. They have to convince their investment committee that this is the best deal on the block. An investment committee is generally an unemotional, analytical group of people who are often generalists with a broad grasp of most sectors. They might employ specialists to help them understand your sector, but these specialists won't be the decision-makers.

Your enthusiastic supporter has to do a big selling job. At the same time, they are not only bringing a deal to the table, but will also be judged on the quality of the potential investment, not to mention how it subsequently performs once made. So, in the institutions, this is very much the start of the next phase, not the end of the first phase.

Here is one really good piece of advice around putting a deal together. If you are looking at individuals investing, then it is better to give them the price and the terms. If it's an institutional investor, then let them make an offer.

> If you are looking at individuals investing, then it is better to give them the price and the terms. If it's an institutional investor, then let them make an offer.

As I said earlier, getting a term sheet or letter of intent is a really good sign, but I have seen deals fall over at the eleventh hour on a number of occasions, which can leave the company facing a very bleak period, particularly if by this stage the money is starting to run out. That's why leaving yourself some more time is ideal. Of course this is sometimes not possible, but it's so important.

Consider again the above example of the company whose simple three-month deal took longer than 12 months. It was only resolved by the company realizing that it was getting into 'not enough time left' territory and giving an ultimatum that the deal be completed in three weeks or it was off. This was really brave with a current investor, but it worked. Only because there was still some time to complete an alternative deal was it possible to have the confidence to do that. It is amazing how quickly an investment committee can be convened to push a deal over the line if needs be.

And here's a revelation that I learned in researching this book. I spoke to an institutional investor who said that if they were putting together a deal with a company that looked like it was going to run out of money, they would deliberately slow down the process and then re-negotiate the agreed terms when the company had absolutely no choice. Nice. Again, this confirms that they only cared about one thing: their money. They did not worry at all about the future relationship – although they did say that, in general, they tried not to 'kill the relationship on the way in'.

Remember, you need to build time into the process.

Negotiating stance

I said at the start of the book that there would not be a specific chapter on negotiation. Here is something to think about, though: who is going to do the negotiating? 'Obviously it will be me; I am the leader', I hear you say. But think about this: a negotiation can get combative and ugly. At the end of the process, if successful, you then have to work with the very same people. You will want/need to have some sort of relationship with the investor that allows for smooth company workings.

My advice would be to work out who in the company management needs to have the least regular relationship, or even the most combative with the investors, and get them to handle the difficult stuff, the things that are going to cause tension. They need to be good negotiators, but a bit of distance from the CEO helps.

There is another benefit from not having all of your decision-makers in the room at the same time. You can always use the excuse of needing to refer to someone else if you are unsure or the decision is a tricky one. It's exactly the tactic we used at PHD. There were three of us, but whenever we went into a negotiation there were never more than two of us at the table.

I have also seen, and actually been, the adviser/chair 'battering ram' doing all of the tough stuff, leaving the founders to enjoy a relatively smooth relationship and transition with the investors. It worked. It meant I was forever the 'bad guy', but I didn't need to work with the investors after the transaction. It's a model that's worth thinking about, as long as you can trust the adviser to understand what you want and what the company stands for.

Using valuation as a negotiation tool

There is one other thing that is worth thinking about, and that is the valuation at which you want to raise the money. I can hear you all shouting 'as high as possible'. I am now going to tell you why that isn't always the best case.

The natural reaction is to price the valuation high. This is because you don't want to be over-diluted. You want the investor to get as small a shareholding as possible. You still want to be in charge. But the higher you pitch it, the more risk the investor will feel they are taking.

As was mentioned earlier, your very first investors (the friends, family and fools) will almost always invest at an inflated valuation. Most start-ups will be valued at a level that is hard to justify with cold, hard data. The valuation is generally based on an idea, a lot of enthusiasm and maybe some evidence that someone wants to buy what you might have to sell. It's not scientific, and it usually maintains a considerable shareholding for the founders. But there is a whole lot of hope in this part of the process. The founders' view on value is almost always different to the investors', but at this stage it's a needs-driven game and a relatively small amount of money. A certain amount is needed, and the founders are only prepared to give up so much equity. A compromise solution is generally found.

The people I spoke to about the process fell into two camps on valuation. Founders would want to achieve as high a valuation as possible. Everybody else suggested that going for a lower valuation leaves you in a better place for the future. 'Everybody else' included corporate finance fundraisers, lawyers and, of course, investors, be they individuals or institutions. You could quite easily suggest that all three had a vested interest in getting a lower valuation agreed. For the fundraiser and the lawyer, it gets the deal done in a smoother way and, of course, for the investor it is a better deal.

But if you look at their reasoning, it starts to make sense. A lower valuation in their eyes equals lower risk. Lower risk should equal a less-stringent shareholders' agreement.

The preference share/loan note example

Lets look at an example where a lower valuation might help achieve a less demanding deal. Everybody on the selling/advising side cites the example of what a deal really looks like if preference shares or a loan note (sometimes called a debt-to-equity deal) are part of the deal. These are two of the things that you should watch out for and try to avoid, and two of the things that some funds/individuals push quite hard. Let me explain.

When a negotiation happens, the investor is looking to take some of the risk out of that investment. In the early stages the risk of losing your money, as an investor, is very high. It's hard to put anything in place to alleviate the risk but for some that's what the tax breaks are for. As the business builds and confidence comes to the company then you would think that the level of risk would be perceived as being lower. But that isn't the case. You are dealing with different types of investors whose whole job is to make investments that make money. They want to lower the risk of losing their money. In some cases they don't have the advantageous tax breaks to lower the risk. What do they do? They try and put clauses in place that ensure that they are first in line for anything that is left in the business if things go wrong. The two vehicles they usually use are preference shares and loan notes.

Preference shares are exactly that. They give the preference shareholders a preference over all other shareholders, ensuring that they get everything first. For example, if they invest £1 million in a company valued at £5 million (after the money is invested), this buys them 20% of the equity. After three years the business sells for £10 million and the investor gets the first £1 million and then 20% of the remaining £9 million. They end up getting £2.8 million of the total, where logic tells you that a 20% share would get them £2 million. You can see how bad that would be for the other shareholders if the company was to sell for £5 million or less, as the investor would still get their £1 million back, plus 20% of anything else. This is not very risky for an investor if the business stands still or grows, or even goes backwards a bit, and if the business closes down they will get the first £1 million of anything that is left, be it assets, cash or intellectual property (IP) value.

Loan notes are even more expensive to the current shareholders. When money is put into the business as a loan, the money needs to be repaid, as well as commanding an annual interest rate. Using the example above, the investor puts £1 million into the business that gives them the rights to 20% of the company. This money has an interest rate of 10%, paid on an annual basis. After three years, at a £10 million sale price, the investor gets £3.1 million from their initial £1 million. Again, you can see how much they end up with if the company sells for a low number. If it was to sell at £5 million then they would get £2.1 million, which is 42% of the money. The other shareholders might think that they own 80% of the equity, but in reality they don't. Again, an investor using a loan note has first rights on anything left if the company closes.

This is why every adviser I have spoken to has thought it better to settle for a lower valuation and hold onto a real equity share rather than a false headline number.

A lower valuation may mean that the preference share/loan note-type deal is taken off the table.

A corporate finance adviser described the valuation as 'an ego trip for founders', and a lawyer said that 'all a high valuation gives you is bragging rights'. You can see why maximizing a valuation is attractive. It makes you feel good. It's a click up from the last valuation. It puts a mental value on the shares that you hold. In most cases, founders forget those little clauses hidden in the new shareholders' agreement that seriously affect their share of the final proceeds.

Avoid preference shares and loan notes if you possibly can. Both of these are an attack on your very valuable equity and the examples above show what the real costs are. The other consequence of putting these tools into the investment process is that when you come to the next raise, the precedent will have been set: yet another lump of money that will have to be paid back first; your headline shareholding further diminished by someone else barging to the front of the queue.

Other thoughts

One other thing to think about is that institutional investors will come at you with a pre-determined set of rules. These rules will have been set over a range of different deals, based on little more than habit and what they can get away with.

They will see it as a given that they get their money back first. They will assume that an equity share of as little as 10% will give them extraordinary control over the business. As one investor put it, they want to 'own you', no matter how small a minority shareholding they have.

Push back, if the demands are too strong. You will soon be able tell where the red lines are for the investors. And don't forget, at this point they are the keenest they are ever likely to be in terms of wanting to agree a deal.

You can offer a realistic valuation rather than an overplayed valuation. If we look at the two examples used earlier, preference shares and loan notes, in almost all cases offering a 20% discount on the valuation and avoiding the use of preference shares or loan notes would still deliver the same amount, or more, money to the existing shareholders on any kind of exit. It's definitely worth thinking about, and a valuable negotiation tool. Just as important is the fact that these investors aren't viewed as preference investors, but the same as everybody else. This brings us back to keeping as few shareholding classes as possible.

In one tech business I worked in, we definitely lost a deal through an over-aggressive valuation. It was never given as the reason, but once the valuation was agreed at its high level, it was never revisited and became the benchmark for the investors. When that benchmark didn't work anymore then the deal was off, and once the investors had adopted that mindset, no amount of re-negotiating would change it. This put an incredible stress on the timeline of the company to raise money, and brought new consequences as alternative investors didn't want to hear that others had walked away; they didn't believe it was for an explainable reason. They didn't want to look like the fools who had fallen into a bad business.

My feeling now is that if the benchmark had been set lower earlier, then the negative view might not have come into place. It doesn't matter how high the valuation is; if it doesn't generate an investment, it's irrelevant. As a corporate adviser said to me, 'there's always a bump in the road, and an overcooked valuation gives the investor nowhere to turn except to pull out or re-negotiate aggressively and unreasonably'.

One final benefit of a lower valuation is that when you get to the next round it is much easier to set a higher valuation at a reasonable level. If you are scrambling around to justify a small increase in valuation – or worse, setting the level at a lower price – it is really not attractive to new investors.

In reality, you should always be fundraising, even if you aren't. Give yourself plenty of time. Once you have completed a raise then start the next one, even if it's only on an exploratory basis. Be wary of pushing for a maxed-out valuation. Use it as a negotiating chip. Try and avoid deals that give the money back to the last investor first. It's the start of a slippery slope and a two-tier shareholder base.

All aboard the Money Train: Raising money at the right time at the right price

- Remember, fundraising always takes longer than you think it will.

- Once you start fundraising, you should always be in fundraising mode, even when you don't need investment.

- Choose who negotiates what. Think about who will be dealing with who post-deal.

- Never knowingly leave it too late to raise money.

- Don't get trapped into an exclusivity period over-running.

- Use valuation as a negotiating tool and don't be afraid to set a lower level for greater gains.

- Don't get trapped into setting precedents for the future with multiple and/or preferential share classes.

5

Raising money at the wrong time at the wrong price

I wasn't sure where to put this chapter. I hadn't even planned to put it into the book. The previous chapter talks about raising money when you have left yourself a lot of time to find funds. But the world is never perfect and sometimes things happen that you don't see coming. Or you just leave it too late. And sometimes success takes a toll. Yes, you can get into trouble if things go too well! I didn't want this to be the last chapter and to finish on a downbeat. It made sense to follow the ideal with the far-from-ideal.

It's fair to say that it is easy to offer advice when things are going well. As I commented to an esteemed professor on a Harvard management course I attended when we were discussing the Apple case history, 'my mum could have run Apple in the 1980s' – of course, not realizing that an oik from southeast London was talking to a main board member of Apple who had helped to run the company in the 1980s. It went a bit quiet! But Apple's sales were growing at double-digits every month, there was no real competition and it was a very cool brand that people wanted to be associated with. I thought I might have had a tiny point... maybe.

How do you get into the wrong-time-wrong-price position?

I have laboured the point that you must not put yourself in a position where you run out of cash... ever.

What do you do if it all looks a bit of a mess and the main mess is running out of cash? I have laboured the point that you must not put yourself in a position where you run out of cash... ever. But it happens, and it can be no fault of your own.

When there's no time, it usually comes as a surprise, but it is you that needs to come up with a solution. There are usually very few solutions available, and all of them will need to be explored at the same time.

Let's look at why you might be in this position.

- You lost a bit of focus and have genuinely left it too late.
- An investment you were expecting to complete fell through at the last minute.
- You lost a major chunk of income unexpectedly (client loss, client going bust, a bad debt).
- Things are going better than expected but payment schedules are putting pressure on cash flow.
- The market has changed and to survive you need to invest a massive amount in something new that is vital to the company (for example, new tech or product innovation).
- There is a major regional or global economic event.
- It has taken a long time to find anybody interested in investing in your company.
- You have invested in the agreed strategy and the performance of the company hasn't moved. You are therefore burning money faster than planned.

This is not an exhaustive list but it covers most of the bases. Some are your fault, some are market forces and some are just bad luck.

From my experience, the worst position to be in is when an investment you were expecting to complete falls through very late in the day. It's not just that the money has disappeared but, to you, emotionally, the deal was already done. You are then in the difficult position of either going back to people you have rejected before or new potential investors who are immediately suspicious as to why someone pulled out, even if those reasons are legitimate and you have a fundamentally viable business.

One of the reasons a deal might fall over is that an investment committee has decided it doesn't want to do it. Your representative has led the due diligence and submitted the investment paper. With the good investment companies this is usually a box-ticking exercise and in most cases the representative will have talked the investment committee through the process as it progresses so that nothing is a surprise. There are – mercifully – few occasions when an investment committee member has got out of the wrong side of bed or has taken against their own investor representative.

I have had the pleasure in a couple of businesses of having to listen to a sore-headed investment committee member put us all straight on the market that we work in, because 'I had a very bad experience in 1983...' You couldn't make it up. But it cost both of those businesses investment, time and confidence. In one case, it also cost the investor representative his job, as they decided they didn't want to work for a company that behaved like that.

One other reason for a failed deal is that something is discovered late in the due diligence process, or there is a big (negative) change in company performance. Again, I have seen this happen. Raising money is distracting and company performance can suffer. Make sure you don't lose focus.

We will come back to the potential solutions for this a little later.

Do you really want to continue?

First things first. In this situation you have to take a long, hard look at your company and yourself. The very first step is to answer the

> The very first step is to answer the question: is this business worth fighting for?

question: is this business worth fighting for? Do I have the energy to keep going? If we get a bad deal, is it worth all the pain afterwards to make someone else more money than me/us?

There is no shame in letting a business go. As one founder put it to me, 'don't worry about failing as long as you realize fast enough'. They went on to say, 'pride is a real killer in the business world'.

> 'Pride is a real killer in the business world.'

If you are having trouble finding an investor, even though you have spoken to everyone, or you have spent the previous investments and the company hasn't progressed, maybe it's time to say goodbye. It's a very hard decision and business founders, in my experience, are eternally optimistic about their companies. But, as discussed, too many flawed businesses survive for too long. If it's not going anywhere, put it out of its misery before you lose everything, and not just money!

At this point it's worth saying that I have never met a founder who thinks their business isn't worth saving. The decision is usually taken out of the founders' hands and made by the non-investors, the current shareholders/investors or a trusted adviser/chair.

You will feel that you have let down the investors, many of whom will be family and friends. But your health and sanity are more important. Keeping going in order to attempt to get something back for the investors is the worst reason to continue. Deep down, you will know what's right.

The racing analogy

About halfway through a season in racing I was starting to think that maybe it should be my last year. It was costing a lot of money; I was stressing about the performance expectations I was putting on myself. Importantly, I wasn't really enjoying it.

I then had two race weekends in a row that made me decide that enough was enough. At the first race I was minding my own business on lap one of a three-hour race when a competitor decided I should not be in the race and took me out. It wasn't my fault; they were disqualified, but it led to a big bill and a big disappointment for me. At the next race weekend, at Spa in Belgium, I wasn't driving well as the stress of expectation was weighing me down. One of the most amazing circuits in the world, it was a privilege for me to drive, but this weekend it felt like a chore.

It came to qualifying, and the whole team was willing me to do well. Joe's last words to me were 'you can do this'. And, boy, did I do it in style. At the famous Eau Rouge bend I lost control of the car and hit a wall at 153 km/h. Amazingly, I was OK. Thank you, McLaren. But it really made me think hard about what I was doing. Something I loved and had done well at was now not the right thing for me to do. I had two races after this accident, and in the very last race we had a class win and an overall podium. This was the perfect finish and I have not had an ounce of regret since. It was in some ways liberating. All I felt was relief.

I know this is different to a business decision, as there are other things to consider, but in both racing and business you can find yourself in the middle of something that you don't realize is taking a massive toll on you. Continually pushing water uphill is tiring and it's only when you're not doing it that you realize what a tough position you have put yourself, and sometimes your family, in. I have been associated with a few businesses where I have watched the founders carry the weight of the world on their shoulders.

One creative company I worked with had lost close to £2 million in the year before I was asked to help, and that was added to some previous debt. I managed to help it get to a small operating profit, but the debt continued to weigh it down. We tried to sell the business, but the historical debt was a problem.

The business had to make compromise after compromise, producing products that it wouldn't normally make and was definitely not proud of, to keep the cash flowing and to keep the lights on. All

I could see were struggling founders who needed to get out. Their stress-ridden, miserable days, weeks and years were their norm, and they were now used to it.

In their eyes, there was always a big deal or commission around the corner that would save the day. After four years I felt I couldn't help them anymore. The business is still limping along, and the big deal still hasn't arrived, and I don't think it's going to. In my view, it was too big a personal burden to them to keep on carrying on.

The first question is therefore: should we keep going? Or even: should I leave the company behind?

What are the options?

Current shareholders and buying time

If the decision is to keep going and you need money, then there are some things you can do, the very first of which is to approach the current shareholders. They are the obvious place to go. You will probably have some idea of their appetite to put more money in. You will have been in touch through their investment period, or they will be sitting around the boardroom table.

The main question is one of belief. Do they believe that the business has a future and, if so, what sort of future? If it's a short-term glitch then you will be in a good position with current shareholders to get through it.

It's not all bad news; sometimes that glitch can be caused by good things happening. As one adviser said to me, 'no one ever plans for success'.

One founder told me of a situation that they found themselves in early in their development. They had taken investment from a venture capital fund. Sales started to really fly. Because they didn't have very experienced financial resources in the company, they ignored the cash flow, presuming that increased sales would lead to better cash flow. What they failed to spot was that the payment terms to their suppliers were on much shorter lead times than they collected from their customers. They ran out of money and the first they knew about it was when the bank stopped the next salary run. The shareholders could see that the company was in great shape and injected a loan into the business. The founder also injected some serious financial resources into the business. It never happened again. Even success can cause you problems.

If it's a less positive glitch, then it will be a lot more difficult. If you haven't decided to close the business or been stung by success, then what do you do?

If a deal has fallen over late on, you probably don't think that you have current shareholders to go to. You will already have explored this prior to looking to raise funds. They will have made the decision to not invest for one of a few reasons.

- The new raise is too large for them.
- They have run out of money.
- It's not part of their investment strategy.
- They are not sure about the business.
- The tax break they enjoyed is no longer available.

But all might not be lost. If there is a feeling that the business is viable and has a future, then my advice is too buy yourself some time. Go for a lower raise than you were originally looking for. If current shareholders were not involved in the investment that went wrong, then the deal was probably a large amount with an institutional investor. The investment was probably planned to get you through the next 18–24 months.

But a quarter of that amount plus some cost-cutting might get you through to a proper fundraise. It might buy you six months. It also puts a different light on your business. A deal fell over, but the current investors are confident in the business and supportive of it even though the investment is outside their normal criteria. It gives a prospective new investor some confidence. They will still want to know why the deal fell over and they will dig deep to find out why, but there will be more balance in their view of you. As an example, one of the first questions the institutions will ask is: have you been refused investment after due diligence?

If you do go back to your existing shareholders don't expect to get something for nothing. If you truly believe the business is worth saving, and you want to buy time, then you will have to do this short-term deal at a discounted valuation. I think that's fair enough for the investors who wouldn't normally invest. Given that you are only raising a fraction of the money, even a deal at a significant discount will buy you time to get a new deal at a reasonable valuation in place.

You will need to put other things in place. Cutting costs will be number one on the list. Be decisive and don't try and kid yourself. Cutting the most junior people or the biscuit budget won't work. Take it as a chance to reshape the business. Take some (more!) of the pain personally. Lead by example. Remember: this is almost certainly about survival.

> Be decisive and don't try and kid yourself. Cutting the most junior people or the biscuit budget won't work.

The number-one strategy is therefore to buy time. I have seen it work really well and work really badly. When it worked well, the existing shareholders all clubbed together and obtained enough money to buy some time and get the company to the next big round (that they would not be taking part in). They got a good deal at a discounted price and some share rights that would put them on a par with any new investor. The management agreed to delay the planned investment in new resources and used that as the reason for the future larger raise. Most importantly, it bought time.

When it went badly, a deal fell over late in the process. The current shareholders said they would not fund the company and encouraged the management to go and look for more new money elsewhere. The need to survive led to a round of significant cost-cutting, which in turn affected revenue performance. But it did buy some time. Not surprisingly, the company was looking less and less attractive, with a deal falling over, no current investor interest in supporting it, revenue declining and a look of desperation. The current investors waited until the company was on its knees and then did a minimal deal at a valuation of around 15% of the deal that fell through – effectively stealing the company from the management.

Interestingly, both of these examples are from the same company. The moral of the story: investors don't always behave consistently.

Money at any cost

You haven't decided to close the company, you haven't got current shareholders to reinvest, you haven't been able to buy time and you still need money. 'Rock' and 'hard place' come to mind.

Bear in mind that you will now be dealing with investors in a different place. They will be looking for a big deal. They will be taking a risk no one else is prepared to take. They really have got you. There will be virtually no negotiation room from your side. But it doesn't mean that you can't try to make it as good as you can. You will be low on confidence, but that doesn't mean that your lawyer, or friendly advisers, should be.

There is one more thing to think about. When you get to the other side of this deal it is probably going to be the case that it will feel like you are working for the new investor. It might not feel like your company anymore. They will impose their business thinking, even if they haven't worked in your sector. Are you prepared to work under those circumstances? If so, then go ahead, but don't underestimate the change.

Where you can make things better is to put in place a deal that rewards you and the team for future success. If the deal is a real fire sale then it's unlikely you will own equity of any significance. This will add to your feeling of not owning the business. However, you could put in place a significant, tax-efficient share option scheme that kicks in when the investor has got their money back and some. In my experience these are acceptable to most investors. They will want you incentivized, but they will want their money back first. All you need to be convinced of is that you can get the business to the point where your incentives kick in.

There is one final thing you can do if you have any form of revenue stream. I have talked in earlier chapters about making sure that you can run the company on a break-even basis with no further investment. That gets harder as the investments get larger. But if you really have no other choice, see if you can make it work. It will mean more work for you and you will probably say goodbye to some of your fellow founders.

It will be a real slog for a few years. It will be a lonely journey and you will probably need some good luck, but you are still in business and you might find a buyer or different type of investor in the future. What you will need to do is find a way of servicing any debt that the company has built up. Talk to your bank; talk to your investors about the new plan, the new strategy. One or all of them may well feel comfortable in supporting this new route. I have seen it work.

This was another brutal chapter. But what's the point in telling you it will all be fine? It often isn't. These are things you need to know and consider carefully. Personally, I have suffered some of my most stressful business moments looking for last-minute cash. If you can avoid it, do. Take the early deal, even if it isn't perfect or even better; as mentioned earlier in the book, take the really good money even if you don't really need it.

All aboard the Money Train: Raising money at the wrong time at the wrong price

- If you are running out of money, look at all of the remaining options at once.

- Make sure that continuing in business is the right decision.

- Be clear on why saving the business is the right route to take.

- Go back to previous interested investors but expect some very deep and demanding questions.

- Look to existing shareholders to buy some time to reset. Be ready to do a very preferential deal for them.

- It's survival mode, so cut costs – hard.

- Look at the viability of a break-even business.

- If it's any money at any price, try and negotiate a deal with future upside and be clear on what that looks like for you.

6

Be ready for due diligence

The difference between what you believe and what is reality can be funny. When I was racing, whenever I got out of the car, I would always be asked how it went. In the early stages of my racing years, even if I knew I had done something wrong, I would try and cover it up or not mention it. I can hear myself now saying I was 'flat-out through Eau Rouge' at Spa in Belgium. What I didn't realize initially was that the data never lies. The data would very often tell a different story. It felt like data was the enemy.

The motor racing world can measure just about everything for a price. The data we had would measure everything from foot pressure on the brake pedal to a hundredth-of-a-second time measurement. I started to realize that it really helped Joe to explain how I could improve; 'brake three metres later at this corner', 'get on the throttle earlier on this exit' – you get the picture. I realized that data could help me be a much better driver. Data needed to be my friend and would teach me a great deal.

In a business, data needs to be your friend, and it's never as crucial as when a potential investor is looking to do due diligence.

What is due diligence?

Due diligence is when a potential investor takes time to look under the hood of your business. It's almost forensic. They will ask you a lot of questions and expect a lot of answers. It's distracting and very time-consuming for a young business that probably doesn't have a lot of spare resource.

Of all the areas I talked to people about, and of all the areas that I have personally experienced, this is without doubt the part of the process that brings with it the most comment. It's an incredibly emotional process for the business founders and a war of attrition for the potential investor.

> It's an incredibly emotional process for the business founders and a war of attrition for the potential investor.

One thing to remember before you start: due diligence is a two-way street. You need to check out the investors as well. 'Don't be embarrassed doing due diligence on any type of investor' is great advice from one corporate finance adviser. A lawyer said, 'ask for a track record. Good funds/individuals will have confidence in their track record.' In the words of a founder, 'it's important that investors understand the company and its market. Do due diligence on them.'

Due diligence with institutions: It's rational

As with the discussions in all the other chapters, there are differences

> Due diligence is an extended interview, and every single thing you do and say through this period is noted and used as part of the case for giving you the investment you want – or not.

between the individual investors and the institutions. In this case I am going to talk about the institutions first, because if you are ready for them then you are ready for any type of due diligence.

In putting this book together, I learned a lot about how the institutional investors operate in the due diligence process. This was in addition to the experiences I have picked up on the way through.

Here is the main thing you need to know: due diligence is an extended interview, and every single thing you do and say through this period is noted and used as part of the case for giving you the investment you want – or not. This is not just the numbers being 'interrogated and interviewed'.

You need to take it seriously and you need the patience of a saint, the skin of a rhinoceros, the stamina of a long-distance runner and a support system like the Forth Road Bridge. Without all of these things, you will be swamped by the avalanche of information requests coming your way.

> You need the patience of a saint, the skin of a rhinoceros, the stamina of a long-distance runner and a support system like the Forth Road Bridge.

The second thing you need to know is that once you have a term sheet, whilst the lead representative for the investor is really keen to do a deal with you, the company that sits behind them are looking for as many reasons as possible to make the deal better for them or not to do the deal. Therefore, anything and everything is added to the information pack.

The people that sit behind the lead investor are the investment committee and the due diligence providers. We have previously described the investment committee, and no matter what happens in due diligence, without their approval no deal is ever done – no matter what the due diligence team say. The due diligence provider can be based in-house or outsourced. If they are in-house, then they tend to be more thorough as they have to live with the consequences if a deal goes wrong after a fund has invested.

External due diligence providers will often be employed by the investment company and will inform the investment committee about the due diligence process. They are usually an independent business but will probably have worked with the investors for a number of years across a number of deals. They will know what to look for and what the investment committee should worry about. Importantly, they want to look like heroes and will pick on all of the negatives and sometimes be grudging with praise on the good stuff.

You can see already that there is a gang out there looking to trip you up, no matter how positive the day-to-day contact is.

We have talked about the rational stance of the institutional investor, and due diligence shows it in all its glory. Be ready for a long and time-consuming process.

> I was told by one investor that 'investors can be really lazy, so we just ask for everything'.

At the beginning you will be asked for lots of information and back-up evidence. Do they really need all this stuff? No. I was told by one investor that 'investors can be really lazy, so we just ask for everything', and in most cases companies will be so willing to please that they will try and provide everything. You don't have to. The same investor said, 'push back if it's irrelevant or unreasonable'.

Be wary of time delays through this process. A lawyer said to me that what the investors want to do is to get the management 'deal exhausted', and I have seen this attempted on many occasions. The lawyer's view was that once the exhaustion sets in, the company 'stops being inquisitive and stops asking questions'. In their words, 'the funds are continually inquisitive'. Their advice was to 'keep asking questions of them'.

There is also a more sinister reason why some funds might want to use due diligence to stretch the time frame. Once the term sheet is agreed then you will almost certainly be in a period of exclusivity. This means that you are only talking to one potential investor. The other interested parties have now been stood down. Exclusivity usually lasts for two to three months and in that time the investor will promise to have completed due diligence and put in place the necessary legal documents. Spoiler alert: it very rarely happens this way. Because it always takes longer.

The feeling from the investor is that once you are in that exclusivity period it is highly unlikely that you will close down the exclusivity at the end of the designated period. You will be far enough through the process to see that things are progressing and will be convinced that the deal is nearly done. You might also be getting to a point where it would be very tight to put in place an alternative investor and you would have to explain why the deal has fallen through.

One suggestion I would make is to ask for a 'still committed' statement on a regular basis – not just a thumbs-up emoji on your mobile every Friday but a proper signed commitment. It will really focus the investors' minds, and hopefully give you piece of mind.

I have definitely been in the position where the company I am helping has reached the end of the exclusivity period without the deal completing. It's uncomfortable but you have to be confident and not just roll over. Withdrawing exclusivity is a very powerful tool. The investor has already spent a lot of money and will not want to waste it.

Stop being grateful and start behaving like you would in every other part of the business. In a deal I was involved in, the time was dragging on and on. Eventually we gave the investor three weeks' notice to get it done, or we would go elsewhere. Amazingly, the ink was dry three weeks later. I am not claiming to be a hero here; we should have done it much earlier.

Once into exclusivity, if you are not careful the initial investor will feel that they have now got you where they want you: relying on them to get the deal done and give you the money you need. And that's where some funds will drag their feet. The reason? So that they can re-negotiate the terms at a point when you have no choice.

As an institutional investor said to me, 'you must remember that the first thing we want is our money back', and then, 'we want to own you'. But the good news is that 'we don't want to kill the relationship completely on the way in'. Well, that's alright then!

> As an institutional investor said to me, 'you must remember that the first thing we want is our money back', and then, 'we want to own you'.

This doesn't happen every time and I am not saying that all funds behave to this extreme. What I am saying is that 'deal fatigue' and the inevitably stretched timelines are not your friends. Being rational and having to continually prove how well they perform will mean that the funds will do whatever they need to do to get the best deal they can for their investors.

The 'interview'

Earlier, I talked about due diligence being an extended interview. What does that mean? The early meetings you have will always feel like an interview anyway. It's normal, as the investors are on a fact-finding mission. They will also want to start to understand the leader/s of the business and how the senior managers work together – in other words, the team dynamics.

Do not underestimate the importance of the 'Can I pop in for a quick coffee?' or 'Do you fancy a beer?' conversations. They want to dig a bit deeper and hope that you will be indiscreet. And not just you, but your team members as well. They will also look at LinkedIn and your social media pages – anything to add to the file. As an aside, this also continues after any deal is done, so beware. It might cost you your job or a re-negotiation at some point in the future.

> Do not underestimate the importance of the 'Can I pop in for a quick coffee?' or 'Do you fancy a beer?' conversations.

All of this sounds a bit bleak, but it is the reality and if you know this then you can plan in advance. There will always be periods during due diligence when you feel a bit exposed. But be reassured, good companies with good systems and information will always be wanted by investors, and showing how well organized you are through the due diligence process will give you a big tick in the box from any investor.

Preparing for due diligence

> Make sure you have a really robust non-disclosure agreement in place.

When you are preparing for due diligence the first thing you must do is to make sure you have a really robust non-disclosure agreement in place. This basically stops anyone from the investor side sharing anything about your business with anybody else – or it *should* do. Spend money on a good one, not a general solution from the internet. Back to the good lawyer.

You will probably have signed one earlier in the conversation, but make sure that it is not one-sided. Get your lawyer to check it if it is provided by the investor, or preferably get them to sign yours. You are about to let them see every detail of your business. Of course, you have to trust them, but it's good discipline and it could stop them sharing information if the deal doesn't happen. I can remember an example from one business that I was leading where one of the current investors announced that they had just put funding into a direct competitor and that they would be the board representative for this new investment. You can imagine how many legal documents then needed to be exchanged around that set-up.

Let's start somewhere close to the beginning. One company founder in the MarTech delivery space said to me that their first due diligence process was a nightmare. They have since had three more as they have raised money in a very successful growing business. What they did say was that the first due diligence 'made them a much better business'. Prior to it, 'we had no grasp on our financial modelling and no idea where everything was'. He continued that 'due diligence taught us how to be a better business'. The problem with this, of course, is that learning how to become a better business through a due diligence process is probably not ideal. You need to be the best you can prior to the process, and most young businesses don't place enough value on being in good shape. They are too busy doing their business to worry about systems and filing.

When I get involved with early-stage businesses, I always suggest that they do things in a way that would withstand the heat of a due diligence process.

Set up a data room

Part of the due diligence process will be to set up a data room. A data room is today a virtual room where all of the key documents relating to the company are placed. Why wait for a due diligence process to set one up? Create one, or something like it, very early on and populate it with all of your legal documents (such as articles of association and shareholders' agreements). Include anything to do with intellectual property, staff remuneration agreements, all of your agreements for office equipment and contracts with your clients.

> It might not fit with your 'laid back' culture, but it will save a lot of time and say a lot about you when people come looking.

Make sure that you have regular board meetings and that you take minutes that are then put into the data room. It may seem laughable and overzealous at this stage and it might not fit with your 'laid back' culture, but it will save a lot of time and say a lot about you when people come looking. It may also make sure a deal gets done.

If there is some doubt about who owns a piece of intellectual property that is key to your offering, the deal may well not happen. One founder told me, 'we couldn't find the designer of the company logo and had no paperwork to say who owned it. After scouring the world, we found him on a beach in Malaysia, but it took a month.'

With regards to the finances of the business, take them seriously from day one. Get the best help you can afford. Talk to other start-ups about what they have done. Good financial management is a really big tick from the rational investors – and, by the way, it really helps you run your business properly.

As an aside, financial management is an area that is constantly undervalued by young businesses. The 'bean counters' are seen as an unnecessary cost that 'bring no value'. My experience tells me that the right financial resource is an investment that pays for itself in about ten minutes. And when I work with young businesses, I strongly encourage them to invest in this space as quickly as they can. I have seen the instant benefits it brings.

It's much easier to set up a data room today, as everything is recorded electronically and there really is no excuse for ignoring this need. When we first set up PHD there was still a lot of paper flying around as the channel of record. Back then, we really did need a physical room full of filing cabinets. But one of my partners was particularly diligent in having a place for everything.

Show that you know your business

In due diligence, above all show that you know your business – not just the big, broad stuff but the detail as well. As an investor said to me, 'investors expect you to know more than they do', although he also said that it would be fair for companies to expect 'the investor to understand their market'. One of the biggest deals I was involved in was with a private equity company that simply wanted to be in the tech sector we were in. It was the first deal for the lead negotiator for this company and they were very overexcited about us. Almost no matter what we said, they still wanted to do the deal. But it was very clear that they didn't really understand what we did and, in some ways, seemed to just want a shiny new thing. The deal happened, but it didn't end well.

When due diligence does start, try and make it one person's job to coordinate everything. Have a point person. By the time that you are dealing with institutional funds, in most companies, this will be a senior finance person, be they full-time or a part-time hire. Get the lines of communication agreed. Let that person drive the flow of information.

Very often the CEO wants to front everything. Whilst who they are and how they lead is really important, they are often not the best placed to answer the questions being asked. A CEO who is vague and ill-informed is a very bad look. Delegating to the right people is a sure sign that the leader is in charge and able to work with the team.

Never lie in due diligence and don't hide anything. The truth will always come out. If you don't know, tell them you don't know. If something surprises you about your own business, then

> Never lie in due diligence and don't hide anything. The truth will always come out.

be surprised, try and work out how it happened and then explain it. As one founder said to me, 'you can't just bluff your way through it; they see through it and often their opinions are very valid'. Remember, you are being interviewed and character is part of that interview.

Also remember these people are from the rational space. It doesn't make them bad people – just different people that need to be respected.

Get ready to do due diligence on the process and your investors

There are some things you can do to prepare yourself for due diligence. As I said earlier, talk to other companies that have been through the same process, particularly those who have worked with your chosen investors. They will be very willing to help and will certainly tell you where they went wrong and what to look out for. There are some more practical places to go. The internet is full of advice and examples. More specifically, the British Venture Capital Association (BVCA) has a range of example papers on its site. One lawyer told me that 95% of funds use these papers as templates and, to his knowledge, no companies that are seeking investment ever look at them in preparation. If you look, then at least you will know what's coming. It will help you to understand and to identify what you need to educate yourself on.

What to expect in due diligence

> I remember being asked for profitability per square foot in one round of due diligence. When we asked why they needed to know this, they didn't really have a very good answer.

The avalanche of questions arrives, and you start working your way through it. It looks daunting but if you are well organized then some of it is a box-ticking exercise and forwarding information is all it takes. The investor will ask you to set up the data room. If you already have one, then that will really help. Agree a date by which no more data will be added to the data room. This will help keep momentum in the deal.

They will want to see all the legal agreements around the company from set-up, all the financial information, contracts on assets, client contracts, property contracts, employment contracts – anything that affects the company and quite a lot that doesn't. Push back if a request is ridiculous. They will have asked for everything, knowing full well that they don't need everything. I remember being asked for profitability per square foot in one round of due diligence. When we asked why they needed to know this, they didn't really have a very good answer. We said 'no'.

As one adviser summed it up: 'control the process; be very well prepared; get the customer and management references ready; get management properly prepped; push the timetable; don't lose momentum; get ready for long days and motivate your team to push the deal over the line; think in advance about what questions they could ask; shut the data room on a set date; push back on stupid or unnecessary questions; continue to speak to your deal champion from the investor'.

All of this is logical and pretty straightforward, unless you can't find that photocopier contract from ten years ago. Where it starts to get more testing is in the personal areas. Do not allow it to get to you and do not get emotional. In the investors' eyes it's another set of boxes to tick – even if, as one adviser described it, the personal questions can make you feel like 'an incompetent criminal'.

There are so many examples here. I have been asked to list all of my personal assets, including savings accounts, investments and property. They said it was to 'try and understand how personally motivated the members of the team are for success'. Personally, I thought it was none of their business. At the time I gave them the information because I was too willing to please. If I were doing it now, I would say 'no'. On another occasion the whole management team was asked to complete psychometric tests. Again, the request was described as helping the investor to understand the team dynamics. Both felt like personal invasions. I hated it.

There will be a lot of questions around events and your management style, often asked in a very blunt manner that you will take as an accusation. How do you react?

Here's some advice I was given. I was a witness in a High Court trial where one of our client companies was accused of passing-off by another. (Passing-off is a legal term for trying to offer a product that looks the same as another in all forms.) I was a witness for the defence and the advice I was given by our barrister was to just answer the question. If it's 'yes' or 'no', then 'yes' or 'no' – no 'buts' or 'howevers'. The questioning counsel were slightly flummoxed by my performance and I was soon off the stand. My advice: just answer the questions and don't get emotional. This is very easy to say and very hard to do.

There will be lots of conversations about theoretical situations. They will outline behaviours that you wouldn't even have in your headspace, let alone think of doing, all causing you to cast doubt on your abilities and character. If the questions go too far, tell them, and then tell them why. But don't get emotional. Answers like 'I wouldn't even think like that' or 'look at how we behaved in this situation; does that suggest we would be that type of company?' can calm things down, particularly in your own head. If you are prepared for the discomfort, then it helps. To you all of it will seem cold and calculating; from the investors' side, it is really just unemotional and rational.

> Just answer the questions and don't get emotional. This is very easy to say and very hard to do.

Due diligence with individuals: It's emotional

Let's come right back to the other types of investors: the individuals and the angel networks. Due diligence with them can be a breeze or a nightmare. The range of due diligence will be from hardly anything to close to the level the institutional investors require. Some will ask for lots of data and may never look at it. They may stretch the time, but in general the lead times tend to be shorter with these investors. They will often be disorganized and, as a lawyer pointed out, 'the worst investors are the non-institutional institutional funds. High-net-worth funds have no discipline.'

If you are organized and clear, that will reassure them that you know more than they do. Which you almost certainly will. They can just get on with loving what you do and taking a tax break on the way through.

This will be the least structured due diligence that you do, but will also probably be the least intrusive and the shortest. It will begin to prepare you for what's coming down the line.

Due diligence is distracting

Due diligence is the most intrusive and distracting part of any fundraising process. Nothing can really prepare you for it and everybody reacts differently.

I don't think that the investment community quite understands how emotional it is for founders and management teams to be interrogated this way, because they only see it from one side. Empathy is in very short supply.

The best remark I heard from a founder about due diligence was the following: 'run the company as if you are always about to go into due diligence'. Getting ready to face it from the start of your business is time well spent and will make yours a better business. The questions will be no less detailed, but you will be in a position to answer things thoroughly and quickly. And don't feel the need to over-supply data. Remember, just answer the question and supply what is asked for.

> Due diligence is the most intrusive and distracting part of any fundraising process.

> 'Run the company as if you are always about to go into due diligence'.

In my experience, in almost every case where due diligence has taken place in a business, if all of the senior managers get involved in the due diligence process, then the distraction always affects the performance of the company, and never in a positive way. This can leave you vulnerable to a last-minute change in terms or scare away the investor. Always have a point person and, if possible, make sure that person isn't the key driver of the company.

Prepare and delegate – whilst easily said and harder to do, this is ultimately the least disruptive way forward.

All aboard the Money Train: Be ready for due diligence

- Run your business from day one as if you are always about to go into due diligence.

- Set up a virtual data room from day one.

- Know your business well, and show that you know your business well.

- Be prepared for an emotional and physical rollercoaster ride.

- You are probably not a criminal, but the questioning will make you feel like one. Do not react.

- Remember that due diligence is an extended interview and that every conversation is part of that interview.

- Do not underestimate the effort required, in both depth and duration. Try to put a time limit on the process.

- Push back if the demands are unreasonable or ridiculous. Investors can be lazy.

- Never lie in due diligence; it will be exposed.

- Try not to tie up all of the company management in due diligence. It's very distracting. Appoint a due diligence 'lead'.

7

Cash arriving is the start, not the finish

The retail opportunities in motorsport are many and varied, and are mostly expensive. There are driver aids, things to make the car handle better or go faster and a whole lot of data recorders to help you achieve just about everything.

When I first got into the sport, I wanted to do things properly and give myself the best opportunities to enjoy some success. Most of the aids on offer found their way into or onto my car, my laptop and my body.

What you realize very quickly is that these things in isolation do not make one bit of difference to the outcome unless they are used, and used properly, and the fundamentals need to be in place for the aids to add value. The car and the driver need to be able to perform in their own right. The car needs to basically be a good car and the driver needs to have some talent.

Putting together a plan

The same can be said of the period following the raising of a cash round. You can raise all the money you need, but you must show that you know what you are doing, that the company is fit for purpose and able to use the funds successfully

You can raise all the money you need, but you must show that you know what you are doing.

and that the management is smart enough to take the business forward to measurable success.

It might seem that a chapter about post-raise behaviour doesn't sit comfortably in this book – that it's not part of the process. If you think that, then think again, because how you and the company behave post-raise will have a massive effect on both your relationship with the new investors and the next round of fundraising. More importantly, if the new investors detect weakness or lack of clarity you will be looking at a whole series of uncomfortable interrogations and potentially a re-negotiation.

Let's go back to the beginning. A basic fundamental when you are looking to fundraise is to know what you are raising the money for. In most cases it's to get more people on board, build the tech, move into a new geography, add a new competence to the business, add manufacturing capability or pay for a currently underfunded element of the business that is expensive. On this last point, marketing is often one of these areas.

> A basic fundamental when you are looking to fundraise is to know what you are raising the money for.

There are a couple of things that investors find very unattractive when looking at investing, including a business's desire to bolster the cash flow or to pay the executives more money. Investors will accept that part of the benefit of the investment can be used for both of these things, but these two together or in isolation are very unlikely to work without a heavy price to pay in the negotiation. The money needs to be spent on something or someone.

You would imagine that having a well-worked plan would seem to be a prerequisite for this, and I would always advocate doing this as it clarifies your thinking and gives future direction to you and the company.

Interestingly, a well-worked plan is not always needed. In my experience it's only once you get to series A with a serious fund, such as venture capital, that the demands for a fully detailed, costed plan are asked for – and even then it doesn't require that much precision.

As one founder said to me, 'be vague on what the money is for. Up to and including series A, you can be vague.' Another said to me, 'in one of our rounds we bluffed, and it worked. We got the money with what was a vague plan. We then used the money in a completely different way. To be fair, it only worked once.' For 'vague' I would say 'a little less specific'.

The reason for this is that having been measured in every way through the courting process and due diligence, a whole set of new measures will probably be imposed for the next stage. And this stage will be over a much longer period than the investing stage. You will be held to account and expected to do what you have said you will do. No investor is going to just write you a cheque with no plan in place and, as I said before, having a good plan will help you in so many ways.

Here are some examples of what to try and get into the plan, without being measurably specific.

- If you are going to add people, don't say 'we are going to add three people in direct sales, two in account management and a sales head'. Say something like 'we are going to increase the headcount in the sales and account management team by about 50%'.
- If you are going to build out the tech, don't say 'we need £200,000 to improve the front end and to hire a developer'. Say something like 'we need to improve the robustness of our tech and improve the customer experience'.
- Don't say 'we are going to launch in the US in three months' time'. Say something like 'we are looking to launch in a second geography and need to do a market assessment and look at the logistics', or even, 'we have a client who wants us to take them to the USA; we need money to explore this option'.

You get the idea. These plans don't sound vague, but are a little harder to put hard-and-fast measures on.

One thing that investors really care about is intellectual property. They will want to be reassured that it is protected (as much as these things ever can be). They will encourage you to spend money on these protections, their logic being that it is a competitive advantage if your competitors can't use what you have. What that intellectual property actually is tends to be of little interest, and in many cases they don't really understand what is being protected.

As you go up the investor ladder to the serious rational investors, they sometimes hire specialists to check on your tech and intellectual property. In almost all cases, none of these specialists know the tech as well as your tech person, and these checks very rarely lead to an issue. However, the protection can be disproportionately important as the investors often ascribe a huge part of the valuation of the business to these elements and their relative uniqueness.

The money changes things; take it seriously

The money has arrived. This is the first day of the next phase of the company and the first thing you need to acknowledge is that it is different. The number of founders I see who think that the money is theirs by right never fails to amaze me. But think about it, you have sold some of your business and it is now partly someone else's as well. It might only be a minority interest, but they deserve respect and access to information. Get your head around this quickly. It saves so much angst and wasted energy fighting the new investor. Don't be dismissive. They may not understand as much as you do, but they are paying money to get you to the next stage.

Board meetings

The first board meeting is particularly important. Everyone will want it to go well, so make sure it does. Prepare thoroughly and don't just rock up and hope it is a success.

What does that mean in reality? There are the obvious things. You will probably have given a board seat to the main investor or someone who represents all of the investors. You might even have two. Treat your board meetings with respect. As one founder said to me, 'learn how to make your board more effective. It should be a decision-making machine, not just a reporting forum.'

The first board meeting is particularly important. Everyone will want it to go well, so make sure it does. Prepare thoroughly and don't just rock up and hope it is a success.

Too many founders and their senior executives see the board meeting as a chore. Use it, and use the board members. Send out well-written, informative papers in advance that are clear and succinct. This then puts the onus on the board to read them and only ask questions at the meeting, without expecting to be taken through every detail. If they don't read the papers, get the chair to pull them up on it. If you make the meeting seem important to you then hopefully they will see it that way as well. Some are just box-tickers. If so, then that might work well for you, but don't take the meeting any less seriously. Make sure the boxes get ticked.

Do not be too willing to please. Over-claiming will only come back to bite you. In almost every company I have been involved in, the CEO always over-claims in board meetings on things like the quality and size of the new business funnel; 'We are really close to signing up all of these clients' – usually listing at least ten prospects.

At the next board meeting, having signed up six, the focus of the investors is always on the four that got away, and not the success of the six. Hence, there is disappointment. Only talk about the ones you have signed up. If the funnel looks healthy then say so, but don't over-promise. It never works.

Sometimes I do feel for the CEO as it's probably the case that the over-claim has come all the way up through the company from the sales executive, who met a friend in the pub... You know the rest.

But don't forget, as one CFO said to me, that a board representative from an investor is 'a walking conflict of interest'. They represent the money, and that doesn't always mean making the best decision for the company. They will always make the best decision to protect their money. Beware!

Board meetings are only one of the ways of communicating with your new investor partners. You will also need to work out how to keep them up-to-date on a regular basis. This will include the early investors, who do tend to get forgotten about when the serious, large players get involved. Don't forget them and stay in touch. Agree a quarterly update for all shareholders.

Sticking to the shareholders' agreement

With the cash arriving you will have signed up to a shareholders' agreement, which is a document that will list the things that you need to get permission from the new investor to act on. It's unlikely that this will be very onerous with the individual investors, but with the institutions it can be a long list. And it's a proper commitment.

It will probably mean that you will have to get permission to make spending decisions over a certain level. This is usually in the range of £50,000–100,000. That will include hiring people and not just capital expenditure. If you do that second geography launch you might need permission to set up a subsidiary. There will be a list of other things that you can and can't do or need permissions for. Learn what they are, ask for those permissions and get written (email) confirmations. And put them in that data room.

The investors put these things in place to protect their investment and to ensure good governance. But if things start going wrong, they can look to use them to trip you up. Give them as few reasons as possible to do that.

We talked in a previous chapter about not going for the absolute maximum valuation. One of the benefits is that you should be able to avoid preference shares or loan notes. Another benefit is that you should be able to negotiate a less stringent list of things you can or can't do without shareholder agreement.

Negotiating this list is important; don't just leave it to the lawyers to sort out. Even the best lawyer doesn't know every nuance of your business and this list can often come at a stage in the negotiation when everyone just wants the deal done. We know that investors never stop negotiating; make sure you don't either. Insist on seeing and agreeing this list. Don't be afraid to push back.

And don't dismiss the lists of permissions. I have seen CEOs behaving as if nothing has changed, even though they have agreed to them as part of the deal. The investor will keep on coming at you if you don't acknowledge the change and act accordingly.

Committing to warranties

You will also have signed up to some warranties. These are things that are put in place to protect the incoming investor. They will be described as disclosures. They normally cover statements such as that the company has never traded illegally, there are no outstanding major tax issues that the company is aware of, that the assets of the business are legitimately owned, that the company hasn't been involved in money laundering or that there isn't a hidden bad debt. These are things that can make a difference to the value of the business or might involve the shareholders having to cover some costs they didn't know about.

What you will be asked to do is sign up to a list of things that you are personally prepared to say have/haven't or will/won't happen. Most investors insist on the entire executive team signing these warranties and, in most cases, there is a personal financial penalty if the warranty is breached. An example would be an unexpected tax bill through some form of previous tax avoidance. You and the team would be expected to pay it and maybe even incur some reputational damages. The total payback is often capped but it's never a small number.

Sounds scary, doesn't it? But it needn't be. You can only sign these things based on your current knowledge. If you genuinely have no knowledge, you are safe. I would also advocate adding to the warranty lists to obtain better terms in other parts of the deal. If you really are sure you haven't done something, then warrant it. These warranties usually stay in place for 18–24 months. Again, check them; don't just trust that the legals are all covered by the lawyers.

Don't leave the disclosures process too late. It can be time-consuming and can often hold up the closing of a deal. For some reason it's often left to the end of the process; make sure you move it up the agenda. Do not send answers to a warranty list without getting your lawyers to review them and don't over-answer. Remember, just answer the question.

Big warning though: I haven't worked in a business that has suffered a warranty breach, but I have seen one from a distance and it was horrible to witness. Most of the executives lost their savings/houses and whilst the business continued there was no trust left between the team and the investors. If you think you can hide something, you can't. Even if it gets through due diligence, it will eventually come to light.

The other warning with warranties is that, rather like the due diligence process, some of the warranties will seem to accuse you of being a 'drug-running, tax-evading, fraudulent forger'. Don't let it get to you. Investors just assume the worst. Good people and good companies don't breach warranties. Use them to help elsewhere.

> Investors just assume the worst. Good people and good companies don't breach warranties. Use them to help elsewhere.

You should also consider asking the investor to warrant certain things, depending on whether they are an individual or an institution. If I was advising you, I would look at this quite closely with individual investors. You probably don't know them, and being the victim of a money launderer is not known to enhance your business – well, certainly not in the long-term! Don't be embarrassed to ask the questions. If they have nothing to hide, then they should have no problem with it.

There are also likely to be a list of things that the investors will commit to doing (or not doing without permission), in either the shareholders' agreement or the warranties. Rather like the CEO who thinks they can run the business as they like, these often get forgotten about. Make sure you remind yourself of these things. The investor won't forget what you have agreed to, so don't let them forget about their commitments. You never know when this will become helpful.

Spending the money

Finally, you will have set some expectations for how the money is to be used and some KPIs to measure the success of these investments. The next chapter talks about setting targets, so I don't intend to get into that here. But let's talk about spending the money.

You will have gone into this whole process in the first place looking for money to spend on things. Investors will be putting money in to help you achieve those things. You are both starting in broadly the same place, albeit with different motivations.

The investor will expect you to spend the money, and on the things they think they are funding. There is no need to rush, but get it done.

There are some cases where the money has to be spent in a certain amount of time. A couple of examples I can think of are as follows.

- The funding happens towards the end of a fund's life.
- There is a structural difference between a venture capital fund and a venture capital trust fund, largely down to tax breaks. With a venture capital trust fund investment, you have to prove that you have spent the money within a certain time frame, which is usually two years.

There are lots of reasons for fundraising but most of them involve funding the hiring of more people. Let's have a look at that. Hiring always takes longer than it should, but don't feel you need to hire quickly. This

> You won't be measured on headcount, but you will be measured on the success of the business after the hires have been made.

is not a numbers game. You won't be measured on headcount, but you will be measured on the success of the business after the hires have been made. Just having the numbers of people in place doesn't guarantee the success. Going right back to my first point, the quality of you and your team and the decisions you make will be what keeps your investors happy. Spending the money and proving the spending works are of equal importance.

An example here. A business in the research space I worked with needed a head of sales. It always seemed to need someone quickly and on three occasions it took on what was available immediately, always hiring the 'least worst' candidate. Of course, none of them worked out; these people were available immediately for a reason. Finally, with some prompting from the chair, and after a small fundraise to pay for it, it went through a complete recruitment process. It took time and the selected candidate had a long notice period. But once they arrived, they instantly made a difference. Revenues grew quickly, the proposition was clarified and the investors could see the difference their money had made. A series of KPIs were ticked off and consequently the investors became relaxed and the chair had a big grin on his face!

One of the mistakes young businesses make on a regular basis is hiring the 'least worst' candidate, or – even worse – the only available candidate. The usual reason is time. Trying to save precious time. In reality, it almost always costs time and requires more money to fix the mistake. One of the worst examples I saw was at a creative tech company where I was a board adviser. A head of sales was recruited, done without the board's approval and presented as a *fait accompli*. It was also announced just before the hire turned up. I knew this particular individual and they knew me. I expressed my reservations, but the CEO was not listening. Nine months later the hire left, having cost several hundred thousand pounds and delivered nothing. Worse, the company had wasted nine months, which had turned into 15 months by the time a new hire was made. It also required a new round of funding as the company had not grown during that period, the terms of which were pretty draconian. Not surprisingly, the board were fully involved in the next hire, imposed severe restrictions on the CEO and lost some faith in them.

Don't do it. Look properly and take the time it requires to make the right hire.

In general, treat any raise as though it might be your last, because it might be. Be bold but not reckless or rushed. Make the best hires you can. But most of all, prove that the investment is working and tell everyone about it. It will serve you well and make you feel confident in your decisions. And you have the right to be confident; you have just convinced some smart people that you and your company are worth investing in.

Rationals versus emotionals

I haven't really talked in this chapter about the difference in expectation between the individual and the institutional, the 'emotionals' and the 'rationals'. I have tended to focus on the institutional. As in previous chapters, they tend to be more organized and more likely to impose measurable KPIs. They will look at the data rather than that month's numbers.

The arm's-length individual investors are perfect, though. They will leave you to get on with it as long as you keep them informed, which, again, is good governance. They will trust you to get it done. There are, of course, the direct opposites, the 'running around with your hair on fire' brigade, panicking at the slightest deviation from the agreed plan they have in their head, which has probably changed a few times and is very different to the actual deal. They are hard to manage, hard to disengage from and incredibly demanding. If they weren't rejected in the selection process you will have to deal with them or get your chair/adviser to calm them down.

Whichever type of investor you have, when the cash arrives, it changes businesses and founders. That should be the case. If you want everything to be yours just for you then don't go looking for money. Nothing comes for free. There will always be strings attached and investors can use those strings to tie you and your business up in knots. It's part of the growing-up process and if you are smart you will embrace and learn. Above all, make sure you spend the money on the things you said you were going to.

> There will always be strings attached and investors can use those strings to tie you and your business up in knots.

All aboard the Money Train: Cash arriving is the start, not the finish

- Accept that it's now less of your own company and that things will change.

- Set yourself reasonable targets that don't trip you up later on. Some of these targets can be less specific.

- Make sure you spend the money on what you said you would.

- Use board meetings to help the company move forward. Make them important and a communication channel.

- Make sure all shareholders are kept informed. Investors do not like surprises.

- Do things at speed but not in haste.

- Hire the right people, not the 'least worst' people.

- Make sure that you know the terms of the shareholders' agreement and the warranty list and get the permissions you need when they are required.

- Remember that shareholders' agreements and warranties work both ways. Make sure the investors do what they said they would.

8

Take targets seriously

I have always been a person who likes a target to aim at. The feeling of achievement when you hit that target never fails to give a buzz.

When I was racing, Joe, my pro driver and coach, would always be setting me targets to achieve. He knew me very well as a person and as a driver. His target-setting was always on the tough side of realistic, but when I hit them I felt amazing. And when I beat them Joe usually went very quiet, which was also a joy.

The targets would be for the obvious things like qualifying lap times, race lap times and average times across a race duration. The hardest targets I had were to try and be within 2% of Joe's times in qualifying, initially for my best race lap and eventually across a race duration. It probably took me a season-and-a-half to get there. But once I did, I stayed there and finally felt like a proper racing driver. One other effect, which Joe admitted to, was that it made him work harder as well.

He also said that if I hadn't taken his targets seriously, or had just come out with a raft of poor excuses, I would have had to look for a new pro driver. I learned that targets were important and they are very important in the investment world.

The financial targets are the most important

You have been through a lot. The money is in and you are now getting on with running the business again. Although you might be thinking about the next fundraise, focusing on the business and getting it to be the best it can be is top of the priority list.

You will have agreed some targets with the investors. These targets are the proper targets and you must achieve them. These targets are almost certainly finance-based, probably around revenue generation, monthly cash burn or gross margin or annual recurring revenue. There are other criteria, but they are very rarely about soft measures. Remember, they only care about their money.

These targets will have been agreed on the way through the investment process. Most conversations will involve a three- to five-year plan, and most investment agreements will have a clause that will cover re-forecasting to a new target, provided that it is approved by the board and the investor/s.

> These targets are the proper targets and you must achieve them.

In reality the days of three-year targets being accurate are gone. I think it's difficult to get things spot-on for anything more than 12 months and for some digital and tech businesses that feels like a lifetime. You will probably be re-forecasting a couple of times per financial year. It's good governance to do that and will be expected of you.

When raising money in the later part of a company's life it can be a bit different; you should have a lot more data about your business, more business knowledge and a revenue flow to give you an idea of your own market size. The forecast should be a bit more predictable and open to less variance.

Things change in the deal process

The investors will talk early on about what sorts of returns they are looking for from their investments and you will listen and do your very best to shape your three- to five-year targets to fit these criteria. And you will probably agree these targets well in advance of the deal completing. If you are not careful, they will become set in stone and even if the money doesn't arrive for another six to nine months, they will be the targets that you have agreed to. So, think very hard about what those numbers look like. Make them as realistic as possible and reserve the right to change them if the process drags on, or even put in a range of targets for the periods.

You might have a stellar sales growth across a 12-month negotiation period, or shit happens. Higher growth might get you to a higher valuation; a dip might put pressure on achieving future years' targets.

In reality you will probably only ever want to change the numbers downwards. But if either of these happen, one side will want to talk about it. I suspect you can guess who is on which side of the discussion! If a right to reset or a range is set early on it may not lead to a late re-negotiation.

Fundraising is undoubtedly a distraction to any company. On pretty much every fundraise I have been close to, I have seen the senior team drawn into endless meetings or answering information requests. And what happens? The company starts to suffer. Revenue doesn't quite reach where it should have been. A key person leaves. A market change hasn't been spotted. A key client feels neglected.

Most institutional investors see this all the time. They aim off for it when they are putting their deal together. They will have a worst-case scenario in their head and provided you stay above that you should be OK.

Whatever you do, make sure that you go into year one with achievable targets. Being behind from day one is a dreadful place to be.

> Whatever you do, make sure that you go into year one with achievable targets.

Investor priorities

Why are the targets so important to the investors? In earlier chapters we have talked about the funds being financed by their clients. They have to perform and report the results. They have targets too, and your targets will be sitting in a spreadsheet somewhere adding to the overall performance of the portfolio.

What you may not know is that these funds often miss their targets too. If you talk to most institutions they will tell you that for every ten investments they make, four will lose them their money, four will make a return of some of the money or break even, one will make some good money and one will really fly and pay for all the losses and build the profit of the entire fund.

They don't expect every company they invest in to make the targets. There is an expectation that some won't. But you want to make sure that you are one of the ones that does. If you do, you will be left alone.

Does this vary between the individual investors and the institutions? Yes, it does. The institutions will have a lot more rigour and will constantly measure. They will also have everything documented and will refer to it if they need to. The individual investor may not even require you to set targets. But this lack of demand will only show itself in a more emotional way if things start under-performing.

The individual is often someone who is generally familiar with the market but may not understand all of the workings. This can mean that they will leave you alone through the tough times, only giving help when it is asked for, and will be supportive and helpful to get you through it. On the other hand, they can decide they want to impose themselves and help you to run the company, saving you from yourself. You know which one you want.

Hit the early financial targets

The advice I always give to any business with targets to hit is to make sure that you hit the first year's target, and hit it well. This gives confidence to the investor and will buy you some goodwill if things start to slow up a bit in future years. Set realistic targets for year one. It's better to over-achieve than to under-achieve. You are trying to build trust and confidence.

Targets are usually measured on a monthly basis. If you miss a month, all the types of investors will want reassurance that it's a blip and things are going to recover or, if they aren't, 'what you are going to do about it'. Miss a second month and then a third and you will be in the full glare of the investor spotlight. They will be all over you, wanting to know everything about everything.

One institutional investor said to me, 'you have to understand that the deal leader works in a very macho environment. They want to look good in front of their colleagues. At best they want to look like they are fixing it.' A founder of an AdTech business backed this up when he told me that if you miss targets consistently, in the investors' eyes 'it's always the fault of the company management, and not a bad investment decision'.

There are also some knock-on effects from consistently missing targets; it makes board meetings very tetchy and it isn't good for company morale.

Do not try to buy time by stopping communicating. Bad news needs to travel at the same speed as good news.

One opportunity to buy some time is if you have a well-thought-through plan that leads to a better-looking future. Take that to the investors before they ask for it. Even if it's not pretty, it will demonstrate that you are on top of it. As an institutional investor said to me, 'investors are generalists; they expect you to know more about your market than they do'.

> Do not try to buy time by stopping communicating. Bad news needs to travel at the same speed as good news.

Let's look at some examples of companies hitting and missing targets. I gave the example earlier in the book of a business I worked with that closed down in 40 minutes. It was a result of the world economic crisis in 2008, which happened four weeks after a massive debt-laden private equity investment deal was done. The economic crisis affected everybody globally and so the company got some leeway from the investor on its targets for about 18 months. There were signs that things were improving but then it lost its biggest client through no fault of its own. It was the financial hit that the investor used to pull the plug. A world event bought some time; a local event was not allowed for. As the investor only cared about their money, they took it when it was there. They just waited for 18 months to find the right time to get it back.

In another example, a business that I knew had completed a major fundraise about a year before a massive global event, a pandemic. The money was to be released in staged payments. The last investment payment was due during the pandemic period. The company was actually doing OK, but was not totally unaffected. Through prudent planning it downrated its monthly targets to a flat growth period, effectively putting the company on hold financially for six months. This was a business that had been growing monthly at double digits, beating all of its original targets. Despite the company being in good health and miles in front of its targets, the investor representative had to fight really hard with his investment committee to not attempt to re-negotiate the terms of the deal for the last tranche of money, which had already been agreed. No targets had been missed but the investment committee saw an opportunity to improve its end of the deal. I don't think the investment committee had a higher valuation and easier terms in mind! Even a global crisis was not enough to get an investment committee to fulfil an agreed deal easily. The fact that the business was not up against it financially worked massively in its favour.

> 'Stand your ground on targets; don't succumb to investor pressure.'

Finally, here is an example demonstrating how the early establishment of a track record really helped. As part of a staged buy-in, a business I was involved with sold part of its equity to an investor. There was a target to be hit for the management to achieve their maximum payment. The year one target was easily achieved. Year two got off to a slow start and it soon became clear that the target was going to be missed by a margin. By the end of month two of year two, the management had re-forecast, changed strategy to a new business focus and presented it to the investor. They were monitored but left to get on with it as the new targets were achieved and the business entered year three in good enough shape to achieve the original year three target and make up some of the shortfall of year two. Having hit the target in year one, there was trust from the investor that bought some time to fix things without huge investor-driven restructuring. The senior management also kept their jobs. They had a track record.

Here is one final piece of advice on targets. The funds will want to market your success so that they can reassure their investors and build a case for their next fund. The better you perform, the higher your value and the higher paper valuation the investor can report. Beware the investor who wants to increase your paper value by setting tougher targets. Stick with either the original agreement or a revision you are comfortable with. Stand your ground on targets. Do not succumb to investor pressure. The old targets get very quickly forgotten if the new ones are regularly missed. It puts a question mark against your judgement and can be hugely dispiriting. As one institutional investor rather surprisingly suggested, 'stand your ground on targets; don't succumb to investor pressure'.

Smashing the targets

We have talked a lot about making sure that you don't put yourself in the firing line. What about planning for success? What about beating the targets?

The first thing to do is to make sure that there isn't a cap on success. If there is, then make sure it's a long way above what you think is possible. Don't let the investors benefit disproportionately from yourself and your team. Make sure that if things go really well, beyond any initial thoughts, you share in that success. If you don't, then you will start to resent the investor shareholders and the business will suffer.

There is an example of planning for success that is comparable but relates to a sale and not an investment. However, it makes the point. When we sold PHD we had an extended payout based on performance over five years. It's called an earn-out, whereby we received some of the payments over an extended, target-driven period. When we did the deal, to be honest, we thought the targets for years four and five were going to be impossible to hit, and we were happy with what years one to three delivered us. We were very lucky; our earn-out was during five very high-growth years in the economy. By the end of year three it was clear that we were going to easily achieve the targets for years four and five and then some. But in the original deal there was no incentive to beat the targets. Fortunately, as it was a trade investor, we were able to re-negotiate, but many funds would not have let that happen. They would have taken all the upside for themselves, putting your loss down to poor negotiating. Give yourself some serious headroom, even if it looks very unlikely that you will need it.

There is one final point on targets. When you raise money, the proposed targets will find themselves into the agreed investment legal papers. For future rounds of investment with new investors, it is likely that they will want to see those papers. If there is a major variance between the targets and the achievement there will be questions around the numbers. Good answers will impress the prospective investor. Hitting those targets consistently will impress them even more.

Targets are really important. Another of the things you must do is hit them consistently. You will then stay out of the spotlight for all the right reasons and you will find that board meetings turn into board calls as the investors focus on more pressing issues with their other portfolio companies.

All aboard the Money Train: Take targets seriously

- Targets are there to be hit. Make sure you take them seriously.

- For all investors, the financial targets are the most important. Pay attention when they are being set.

- Deals can take time to complete; build in some flex or re-forecast room if the time runs on.

- Give yourself every chance of hitting the year one target.

- Make sure you communicate with the investors. Bad news needs to travel at the same speed as good news.

- If you need to re-forecast put together a plan and get to the investors before they ask for it.

- Plan for success as well. Give yourself room to benefit from over-achievement.

9

A deal's a deal

In the previous chapter I talked about how my pro driver Joe would set me targets when I was racing. I also talked about the thrill of achieving those targets. What I didn't talk about was what happened if I missed those targets or, worse, was seen as not trying to hit those targets. In Joe's eyes those targets were an agreement between us. In his world, he wakes up every day and has to be the best racing driver he can be – no excuses, no 'feeling under the weather', 'the car isn't set up right'. He looked at me and saw a racing driver and not a hobbyist achieving a lifetime dream.

I learned the lesson very quickly that if I agreed to a target or a strategy, I had better achieve it or try my hardest to achieve it. The team and Joe were expecting, and I had better deliver – no soft excuses or looking for understanding. A deal's a deal.

The important thing was that the targets were mutually agreed and understood, and not dangerous, hidden, ambiguous or a straitjacket.

It's similar to taking on an investment and the deal that comes with it. You must embrace it, or be seen to be embracing it. Unlike a passion such as racing, if you fight it and fight it unreasonably then the exit door awaits. And that's the exit from everything you have built.

What you can and must do is make sure you understand what you are signing, understand what it commits you to and push back before the deal is done. Because you won't be able to do it afterwards.

Know your deal

The last chapter looked at the financial targets that you have agreed to achieve. This chapter is much more about the details of the deal paperwork and how not to fall foul of a hidden clause.

This chapter was originally going to be called 'Don't expect understanding'. Most reasonable people behave reasonably. Most investors are reasonable people as individuals but tend to be inflexible once they have an investment committee and their investor clients putting pressure on from behind. They cannot be seen to be weak and under no circumstances can they make a deal look less valuable.

For the company that is being invested in, this almost always means that the chances of re-negotiating a deal are practically nil. Even re-negotiating an investment agreement term is almost impossible. I have been in a room where the intransigent investor has said out loud 'a deal's a deal'. All investors fall into the 'a deal's a deal' category if a change in that deal means that they will potentially be worse off. The only way 'a deal isn't a deal' is if the investor can improve the terms to their benefit. By now you will have understood that this is the institutional investor's job, but it's also the case for the canny individual investor.

What this means is that you need to thoroughly understand the deal you have done. Understand – or, better still, get your lawyer to explain – the terms of the deal until you understand the terms and, much more importantly, the consequences of those terms. And if you don't have the ability or the interest (and trust me, you should have), then make sure someone else in the organization does. The CFO or the trusted adviser/chair are very good places to start.

There are the odd occasions where, after a while, a clause can be working against the future success of the business and therefore the value of the investors' shareholding. It wasn't set up that way, but as time has moved on and markets have changed it's clear that there is need for a change. Not surprisingly, the investors are then happy to make a change. This is one of the few times when changing within the agreed terms works, but that's largely because there is something in it for everyone.

What never works is showing an investor that you don't understand the deal you have signed. You can almost hear them rubbing their hands together.

Watch out for the 'norms'

Earlier in the book I said that I wasn't going to give specific advice on negotiating, mainly because every negotiation is different, and generalizing isn't going to help. But there are some things to watch out for that can be easily brushed over.

Where are the traps? Here are some examples.

It's ridiculous

The biggest things to look out for are the 'norms'. The hope is that you will accept the norms because they are, er... the norms. One investor told me that 'it's ridiculous. We buy into a company and have about 10–20% of the equity and then act as though we own the company. Getting our money back first is a given. We put stringent terms and investment agreements in place. We dismiss them as norms and this positioning never gets questioned. The companies seem in awe of us. They feel like they can't question it. My advice would be to question everything.' I look forward to the next negotiation with him!

> 'The companies seem in awe of us. They feel like they can't question it. My advice would be to question everything.'

But his point is a good one. You need a mental checklist before agreeing to a deal.

- Don't be in awe of the investor.
- Unless they have a big majority equity holding, they don't own you. Behave like they don't own you. They are partners, not owners.
- Don't let the deal put the investor in a position where they do own you – again, unless they have a majority equity holding.

- Question everything you don't feel is relevant or don't understand.
- Get your lawyer to help to identify the ridiculous clauses.

This should improve the deal, as well as into the future, when the deal is done.

We have already talked about an example of the norms, these being preference shares and loan notes. These are not brushed-over terms, easily ignored. Even an average lawyer will raise the issue, but beware of them saying that they are norms, and you should just accept them as normal. Remember, every clause you accept becomes a new norm for future negotiations.

Let's have a look at some other challengeable norms.

Fees

I am always amazed at how many businesses just accept the fees that come with investment. My experience would tell me that here there is a difference in the ways that fees are covered when looking at individual investors and the funds. Individual investors tend to pick up their own legal fees and very rarely ask for any form of investment fees or ongoing charges, unless they take an active non-executive role. The funds, on the other hand, will aim to charge you their legal fees (including due diligence costs) and some will try to charge ongoing annual recurring fees. This would be in addition to your own legal fees.

Let's have a look at how the funds can charge. In most cases the costs of a deal are initially funded by the fund managers, not the investors in the fund. This means that due diligence and legal fees all come out of the management fees the fund charges to its investors. When a deal is completed these charges are almost always then passed on to your company. It has cost the fund managers nothing to look at you and get all the legal agreements agreed and drawn up.

This is why it is rare that a deal falls apart once you are well into due diligence and legals. Any money spent on a non-deal is dead money and hits the profitability of the fund managers, not the investors in the fund.

Fees vary wildly. The smaller funds and regional funds will charge an arrangement fee, which is a charge made by the fund for managing the deal, i.e., paying for their time. This is almost always a percentage of the amount of investment, typically between 1.5% and 3% depending on the size of the investment. On top of that there is an annual monitoring fee, which is a fee the investor charges for making sure that the terms of the deal are adhered to. This is a moveable feast but it's usually tens of thousands of pounds. If there is a board position being taken up there will also be an annual non-executive director's fee. All norms, obviously! Interestingly, the more progressive bigger tech-based venture capital funds will just charge a board fee. Their logic is that the more they take out at the beginning, the less there is to invest in future success. And future success is where the big wins are for them.

But think about it; in the worst case, if you are looking to raise £1 million and you are charged all of these fees, then in year one you could be looking at upwards of £80,000 in fees. This would be followed by an ongoing number of at least £40,000–50,000 per year. Across three years, that could be close to 20% of the money you have raised. Even saving 10% of that figure would make a difference.

It's hard to generalize here. Some funds charge everything they can. They tend to be the smaller funds or regional funds where there is less direct competition for their money. They charge them because they can. Just a thought: if it is a fund that charges fees just because it can, then you might want to think about whether it is the right investor in the first place.

> If it is a fund that charges fees just because it can, then you might want to think about whether it is the right investor in the first place.

But whatever the fees are, negotiate them and get them capped in advance. And push hard to get the number as low as possible. This would also include negotiating with your own lawyer. That way, you know what you are in for. Make sure that you don't agree to pay the funds fees if the deal falls away. It does happen.

Deal fees are always expensive, and most founders don't factor in these fees at all. If you just accept the fee norms, then it will be very, very expensive.

Back to setting the precedent. If you overpay the first time, you will keep overpaying when new investors come in future rounds. Challenge these numbers. It will give you more to spend on making the business a success.

Investor consent

In any agreement from an institutional investor, and increasingly individual investors, there will be an investor consent list. This does exactly what it says on the tin. It's a list of things that you need consent from the investor for before you do them. This would typically be hiring people over a certain salary, not committing to more than a certain amount of capital expenditure, not setting up subsidiaries etc.

A lot of these things will be things that could interrupt the day-to-day running of the company. If the investor only has a 10–20% equity holding, why on earth should they have so much control? To protect their investment? Of course. To make sure you aren't spending it on sex and drugs and rock 'n' roll? Yep. But hiring people? Signing up for office equipment? Really? It's because they have become norms and they just get added to the list.

Challenge the list of items on the investor consent list. The investor will have a standard list and you need to make them justify every clause on that list. I mentioned earlier that this list is often one of the last things to be agreed. Don't let deal fatigue cause you to brush over this document.

Participation rights

Participation rights are another norm. These basically mean that when/if you go for the next round of funding, the previous investor can either invest again up to their 'natural share' or in some cases they can invest the whole amount, as long as it's on the same or better terms than the new prospective investor.

That's great, isn't it? Some competitive tension already built in. A vote of approval from a current investor that they want to participate again, because the company is doing well. If they put all the money in, then it's one fewer investor to deal with. What's not to like? In seven out of ten cases, I would agree.

But what if the current investors have outgrown their usefulness? What if you need investor experience in another geography or market sector? What if the current investor is just so difficult to deal with, and having them as the secondary investor would work so much better? Like a lot of relationships, you can outgrow each other. What was once a mutuality is now a flourishing business held back by a heavy anchor. It happens. If you can, make sure this clause is two-way, i.e., that the investor can only participate if you want them to. It may be totally appropriate for them to go again, but if it isn't, you want to be able to have a choice.

> Like a lot of relationships, you can outgrow each other.

Drag-along and tag-along

Then there are drag-along and tag-along rights – yet another set of norms. To simplify it a lot, these are two different clauses around the same issue. If someone wants to sell their shares, with drag-along rights they can make the other shareholders sell their shares at the same price to the same buyer, provided that buyer wants to buy more shares. Tag-along rights work the other way around; if another shareholder has been offered a price for their shares, then tag-along rights give the other shareholders the right to be part of that transaction on the same terms.

Pretty much every investment contract will have both of these clauses, and they are sensible clauses. The key is to work out how much control you have over the clauses being implemented.

For example, imagine the timeline on an investor's fund is coming to an end. They have achieved their financial goals and they want to cash out, selling their holdings to return the (hoped-for) upside to their investors. They have done their job. The problem you have is that it might be just at a time when the company is flying, and the management doesn't want to sell.

But the investor has found a buyer for the business. Because the drag-along clause is weak, they have implemented the drag-along right. They are going to sell because it works for them. There aren't the funds in the company to buy their shares and it's hard to see where else the money will come from. But they can drag you along as well because you don't have a right of veto. I have seen this happen with an investor having as little as 30% of the equity. You might not want to sell, but you have to. The company has gone to someone else and you now work for someone again.

Two points need clarifying here. The first is that there are not many buyers who want to take on a company where the management is unwilling to sell; second, if the company is doing really well, it's not impossible that a buyer of the exiting investors' shares may be found. Although, as discussed earlier, it is often very hard to find a purchaser for existing equity. It is usually at full price and the prospective purchaser will never be quite satisfied with why the shares are for sale – even if it is for a very good reason.

Try to avoid getting into this situation. It's unlikely you will get a total veto. No investor is going to sign up to a company that is never going to sell. But you might have a clause that says that a big percentage (70–80%) of the equity holders have to agree for everyone to be dragged along. You might also have a clause that gives you the right to buy the exiting investors' shares on the same (or discounted) terms. You might be able to borrow the money to buy them out.

One way of putting these veto rights into the legal papers would be to have some form of overarching clause. It's preferable not to have a long list of veto rights. It takes a lot of negotiating and you are constantly thinking of increasingly unlikely events to have a veto over.

An example of this type of clause would be where you, post-deal, retain a majority share of the equity of the company and insert a clause that requires either a board majority vote or a significant percentage of the equity holders to agree.

Why is all this important?

The reason you need to know the details of your deal, and adhere to them, is that if you do get into trouble and if things turn sour with the investor, the second place they will come looking is to see if you have been in breach of the investors' agreement.

> If things turn sour with the investor, the second place they will come looking is to see if you have been in breach of the investors' agreement.

(The first place will be the financial condition of the company and the financial targets hit/missed.) If there has been a breach, no matter how small, it will be used to claw back or rewrite the agreement, and probably to impose further, stricter, investor consent clauses.

To try and avoid this when the investment is completed, establish an investor consent system. Email is probably the best way to do this. Keep all of the approvals in a safe place – perhaps the data room. Revisit the list on a regular basis (it's unlikely you will carry this list in the front of your mind), make it someone else's responsibility to do this, or make it part of the board meeting process on a quarterly basis by reviewing the list and seeing if you have missed anything in the last quarter.

It's important. I have seen the very best companies forget. For example, I was chair of a MarTech company that was growing fast. A lot of the growth was coming from another geography. It was decided to set up a subsidiary in that market. There was no risk. The board had approved it and the representative from the investor was a member of that board. No one raised the issue of investor consent. And yet, when the list was being checked for something else, there it was in black and white: the company needed investor consent to set up a subsidiary. Permission was then sought and given, six months after the set-up.

It turned out to be hugely important, because three months after permission was given there was a new round of fundraising with this particular investor looking to challenge the company's valuation (downwards, obviously!) and looking for any reason to do it. One of the areas they looked at for a lever to lower the valuation was potential breaches of investor consent. There were no breaches but there could so easily have been.

It's easy to dismiss the list as something that is put in a cupboard and forgotten about – perhaps by you, but not by the smart investor.

The individual investor

Where does the individual investor sit in all this? I have deliberately talked about the most rigid investors, the institutions, but you should have exactly the same discipline when dealing with an individual. With the institutions it will always feel like you will be trying to catch up and know as much about the deal as they do, and most likely it will be their paperwork you are dealing with. With an individual it is almost your duty to know more about the detail of the deal than they do, and it is an opportunity for you to put the paperwork in place. They will behave like a lot of founders do – 'leave it to the lawyers' and 'don't bore me with the details'. This is a good thing, provided you don't do the same.

Individuals who make multiple, regular investments (serial investors) are very smart and will drive the process for you. They will try and impose an investor consent list. Make sure that you employ all of the same discipline you would employ with an institution. Again, beware. Most of the norm areas mentioned above will form part of the final documentation. With the individual investor, try and set the agenda. Offer to produce the legal paperwork; if you can achieve that, you will be in the driving seat. Remember, don't be too grateful and don't just say 'yes' to everything.

Here is an example of how things change. I worked with a very smart CEO who was a brilliant mathematician. He knew every detail of every deal. I marvelled at him as he spoke to investors. They were usually in awe of him by the end of the conversation. It meant that early on he got most of what he wanted in his individual investor agreements. However, with the next raise and the rational funds being the potential investors, they knew as much as he did and were actually a little suspicious of his intellect and his constant smart solutions. We spotted this early, and before trust became an issue it was decided to spread the load across more of the team and get the lawyers to do some of the heavy lifting, under instruction. It worked.

I have tried to cover some of the big areas you are likely to come across. There are many more. And be wary of the clauses that refer to other clauses and sub-clauses. Sometimes there is an override somewhere.

Try and fully understand the relationship between the articles of association and the investors' agreement. It's important which document takes precedent. For example, some documentation I saw recently showed in the articles that 100% approval and signatures from the equity holders were required for a big range of things: sale, restructure, investment etc. However, in the investors' agreement that number was 75%, and the investors' agreement overrode the articles of association. The two biggest shareholders had 74.8% of the shares. The management still had a veto. Good planning!

There will be other areas that you need to look at, but the main piece of advice is to know your deal documentation, and know it well. Adhere to the clauses you have agreed. Make sure you question the norms. And remember, 'a deal's a deal' – and don't expect understanding.

All aboard the Money Train: A deal's a deal

- It's almost impossible to re-negotiate a deal in your favour once it's signed and in place. A deal's a deal.

- You need to know your deal well; love the detail (or get someone else to).

- Do not be intimidated by your potential investors. That's what they want you to be.

- Make sure you understand every clause before signing. Post-signing is too late.

- This is a business of norms in contracts. That doesn't make them right; challenge them and push back.

- If you have investor consent clauses, make sure you get the consents and keep the copies safe.

- Revisit, and refresh your memory of, the deal regularly.

10

Be ready to switch strategies

It's been a brilliant weekend. The sun has shone and the forecast for tomorrow's race day is more of the same. Testing on Friday and Saturday went well. Qualifying was the best ever. Joe and I have agreed on our race strategy. All we have to do is turn up, drive well, and we have a real shot at success.

Except, when I woke up on Sunday morning it was raining. No matter how hard I looked at the weather apps, the rain was in for the day. I had raced in the wet, but not in this car on this track. I had a ten-minute warm-up session three hours before the race to try and get a feel for how the car and I would perform – not enough time, but all the time there was.

A complete change in the way I needed to drive and a complete change in race strategy was required, all of it unexpected and with nowhere to hide. During the race it took a little while to get there, but by the end of the race I was on the pace and doing OK. The other amateur drivers were having similar issues. It was about who could adapt the quickest. Having a knowledgeable pro to guide me through it was invaluable.

Does that feel like business life for you? You are told to expect the unexpected but it's still a shock when it happens. How you respond is the measure of you and your company. Investors will judge you when a change in strategy is needed.

The need to adapt

How many times do you see a business flying in a market with seemingly no real threats to their success? You might even be in one of those businesses right now. Or you might be in one that used to be like that.

Things change, and they can change very quickly and unexpectedly. Markets evolve, products change, opportunities come from left-field, threats present themselves and competitors catch up. Or what you are offering needs to be served up in a different way. All of these, and more, mean that something needs to happen. It probably needs to happen fast.

It seems to be a truism that all founders believe that their business is the best there is and they can't understand why the whole of the rest of the world can't see it. You know it's true. Sometimes the rest of the world just needs a bit of time to catch up! And sometimes you need to change to catch up with the rest of the world, and to do it quickly.

If you do need to change, how do you get your investors to change with you?

In the previous chapter we talked about 'not expecting understanding'. This was focused on trying to change a deal, or not fully understanding the deal you have done. Being ready to switch strategies is very different. This is about looking after or enhancing the future of the business, not about trying to gain something from the deal.

When the investors have put their money in, as described, they will have done it against a set of targets and probably a three-year financial plan. All has been agreed and all the company now needs to do is go ahead and achieve, subject to a couple of re-forecasts a year.

But through that period things happen, and markets change. And a good majority of things that happen are really good opportunities, not threats. There are so many things that happen that can offer an acceleration opportunity or the chance to move into another market or another geography, or to change your pricing policy or extend your tech. These can offer a real chance to become more successful. These opportunities weren't there when the deal was done. You don't know what you don't know.

Talk to your investors

Both opportunity and threat need to be addressed with your investors, and they need to be addressed by you before the investors spot them. Remember, they are generalists who expect you to know more about your market than they do.

It should almost never be the case that the investor spots the opportunity or threat first. The exception would be when it's a trend that will affect you but isn't market-specific. Examples of such are a global financial crisis or a pandemic. If it's an opportunity, then it could be happening in another global market that you don't know. The investor may have a broader view; they may have seen these things earlier through other portfolio companies and will be able to bring their knowledge to the table.

> It should almost never be the case that the investor spots the opportunity or threat first.

If you have spotted something – good or bad – you will need to address it. Ask yourself the following.

- What is the threat/opportunity?
- What do I need to do to grab it/resist it?
- What is the time frame?
- Is more money required? How much?
- What resources do we need to add/lose?
- What is the potential effect on the investors' investment?

This last question is important for one reason; remember, they only care about their money.

As soon as you spot the opportunity or threat or see a trend happening consistently, talk to your investors about it and tell them what you are going to do about it. This would normally involve putting together some kind of review to present. It doesn't need to be finalised;

it could be an interim report with more data needed. This will start the process. Remember, it's not a proposal for re-negotiation; it's a change of strategy.

Given that most of the funds have a wide investment base, they or their fund may well have had experience of similar switches. If they have, it will immediately make them feel part of the process.

One of the hardest sells is when it looks as if you will be going backwards before leaping forwards. This usually involves burning more money and losing revenue. It's risky and will need a very convincing sell. The smart investor will respect a well-prepared plan.

Examples of strategy switches

Let's look at some examples. One was driven by a massive market change, the second by a simple but unnoticed fix and the third by an unexpected market behaviour.

In the first example a CommsTech business I was involved with was starting to build a successful client base. The monthly revenue line was trending in the right direction and all seemed good. Until it wasn't…

Although the product was high-tech, the actual delivery of the product was still a relatively manual process. From nowhere a trend that looked years away happened overnight. In a few short weeks the market shifted to an automated delivery system. The company had seen that it would come at some point in the future and was developing an automated product, but not quickly enough. The company hadn't felt under enough pressure to deliver it.

The decision that needed to be made was whether to stick with the manual system and hope that clients would make an exception or switch all resources to developing and selling the automated product. The company was not a dominant player in the market and couldn't dictate market behaviour.

The investors, who were relatively new to the business, were talked through the situation and eventually backed the company's recommendation to go automated. It meant the traditional revenue line collapsed and it took time for the automated system to catch up. This meant there was a financial hole.

The investors needed to be convinced that the market was in the automated space. They were convinced by the management and the company recovered. The investors had to fund the short-term cash issue, but the company got back to where it had started and beyond. But if it hadn't reacted quickly and brought the investors with it, then I suspect it wouldn't be in business now.

The next two examples are from the same MarTech company. In the first example, a simple fix transformed the company. It had just been through a round of fairly modest fundraising. The CEO was smart but couldn't understand why the product wasn't shifting. After looking at the business and the market, the CEO decided that the product was right, but it wasn't going to sell itself. He decided to go all-in and hire an experienced salesperson who would be paid significantly more than him. His reasoning was that just ambling along, waiting for the world to catch up wasn't working for anybody, including the investors.

This was the first stage of the strategy change to sell to the investors. It meant that the recently raised funds would run out more quickly if it didn't work and that more money would be needed to fund the hire. It also meant having to go through the process of recruiting the salesperson. It was estimated that it would take six months. Six months where there probably wouldn't be much change in the current performance – a big ask of the investors. The plan was presented to the investors with supporting data and well-worked budgets, including what the estimated upside would look like. They bought the strategy, were part of the recruitment process and the hiring was transformational, not just because the new hire was a great salesperson but because the salesperson changed the way the product was marketed and sold.

The CEO did well to spot the weakness in the business and the investors did well to back it. The CEO was decisive and communicated with the investors clearly and quickly. The story also has a happy knock-on effect; when the next round of funding was required, the current investors were first in line to invest.

The next example was driven by surprise market behaviour, concerning the same company as above. With the new salesperson in place, sales moved forward quickly. In no time at all, there was a long client list. The interesting thing was that over 40% of the revenue was coming from a geography that the company had no physical presence in. On looking at it, the reason was that this market was physically huge and clients in this market were used to being sold to remotely.

However, with no physical presence in that geography it meant that customer service (or lack of it) was a potential issue and the significant time difference didn't help. All of this was presented to the investors with a plan to recruit in this new market. It required more money. The figures were done and the acceleration in the company performance was forecast to be huge. The investors could see that their current investment was not at risk and the new investment was to be used to take advantage of an unexpected opportunity at a relatively early stage in the company's development. Ticks all round.

In all the above cases something happened, each opportunity or risk was spotted by the company and all of them reacted quickly. In every example the company made a very good case for the change in strategy. There was a compelling enough story to convince the investors that they would benefit. There was no attempt to re-negotiate the terms of the deal. All investors wanted to continue on the ride and in one case put in more money at the next round.

Talk to your investors

Remember, no one, particularly institutional investors, likes surprises.

There are two things for you to think about. First, if you spot something, don't sit on it; investigate it and talk to your investors. You might decide it's a short-term trend that will pass but give yourself that option. Second, remember, no one, particularly institutional investors, likes surprises. They need to hear it from you, not one of their colleagues who runs another portfolio business or their mate from the city who they met in the pub. As one founder rather dramatically told me, 'people procrastinate about delivering bad news for longer than it takes to deliver and resolve. I have always found it easier to tear the bandage off and get it out in the fresh air.'

Changes in strategy can look very scary, but if they are well researched and evidence-based then they are usually the right thing to do and relatively easy for an investor to accept. This would be true for both taking opportunities and for saving the business. If you are struggling, the investor will probably be looking anyway, so try and beat them to it.

How does the individual investor fit into this? If you think about it, then they are actually more likely to see you make strategic changes, albeit at a smaller ticket price.

When you are early in the life of your business it is unlikely that you will get things absolutely right in the first, second or even third iteration. You are unknown, small and learning on your feet. You will also probably be trying to do too many things at once rather than focus on getting one thing right. The individual investor will have come in early. They will expect things to change. They care about their investment and will not want to be on the hook unexpectedly for more money – 'unexpectedly' being the word; remember, there should be no surprises for the investors.

Unless they have been difficult all the way through – and you will know who they are – it is most likely they will support whatever you suggest, but don't take this as permission not to do your homework properly. It requires the same diligence as for an institutional investor. You are not doing this to just win over an investor. You are doing it to save/drive your company.

It's a strategy change, not a re-negotiation

You have to be very careful not to fall into the trap of making this look like a re-negotiation of agreed terms. This must be a strategic change. If you have an independent chair, run it past them first. If you recruit them to your thinking and they are doing their job, they can often lay the ground for you. If they are seen to be supportive then that will often help bring the investors on board. But be prepared for rigorous questioning. You will need to demonstrate that you understand the issue/opportunity and that you have the best solution.

All of this is doable – not easy, but doable. And almost every business needs a strategy switch in the lifetime of an investor's involvement with a business. Make them an ongoing part of it and they will support and, in many cases, further fund. Right back to the due diligence section, though – this is still part of the interview and the test. As an investor said to me, 'sometimes a question is set to see how you respond, not what you respond with'.

And if they don't buy into your strategy change, then it is for one of two reasons.

- In their eyes, you haven't made the case.
- They are not the visionary investor you need. In which case you will need to look for one who is. Back to Chapters 1 and 2.

All aboard the Money Train: Be ready to switch strategies

- Things happen unexpectedly, both opportunities and threats.

- Spot them and then put together a case for a strategy change.

- React before the investors come to you.

- Remember, it's a strategy change, not a re-negotiation.

- Prepare a proper plan. Have all the answers to the financial questions.

- Make your investors part of the decision and communicate early and effectively. Remember, no surprises.

- Show you know your market better than the investors.

- Take the investors with you.

Summary of the 10 things young businesses need to know about investors

The Money Train is a real thing. it's fast and demanding. Once you are on it then it's a journey that is pretty much defined for you. You will have to deliver a return to the investors who have chosen your business to invest in.

For you, your key drivers should be to maintain as much control as you can for as long as you can, and to make sure that you get your fair share of the rewards – instead of doing all the hard yards for someone else to disproportionately profit from.

You *must* be the main profiteer from a successful business, always accepting that without the investors the business would not have been as successful and as valuable.

As I said right at the beginning of the book, it always seems to me so unfair that the first serious negotiation you do to raise funds is done at a time when you know the least. It is the most influential structural deal you will do. You need to avoid the traps.

I don't intend to specifically summarize all ten things here, but the following are some reminders.

Remember about investors.

- They tend to fall into the *emotional* or *rational* category. You need to understand and respond in the same way. But, in truth, they are all the same.
- *They only care about one thing: their money*, and the multiples it will make through you. It's why they invest.

There are some resources you will need.

- *Finance expertise*. Don't leave it too late to bring on board finance expertise and general management skills. It's an investment, not a cost.
- *A lawyer*. Have the best lawyer you can afford at all times.
- *Advisers*. Have mentors, advisers, a chair, non-execs and founders who have been there and done it; all should be there to guide you through and listen to you.

Remember the following.

- *Decide*. Do you really need to raise money? And how, what and why are you raising it?
- *Prepare*. Run your business as if you are always in the best position to raise money and always be raising money, even when you aren't. It's better to raise too early than too late.
- *Question*. Don't be afraid to ask questions of the investors or challenge their norms. Do not be in awe of your investors.
- *Understand*. Make sure you know what all the legal documents mean and what can happen to the business if things change. And if you don't or can't, find someone on your side who can.
- *Be inquisitive*. Do not run out of energy and fall foul of deal fatigue. The investor will probably out-energy you. Share the load and keep going as long as you can.
- *Keep focusing on the business*. Raising funds is distracting. Share the load and don't try and do it all yourself.
- *Hit the targets*. You have signed up to a deal. Hit those early targets to build confidence.
- *Control*. Through all the deals, be in control of your destiny for as long as you can. You need to be the leader of the crew.
- *Communicate*. Talk to your investors regularly. Bad news needs to travel at the same speed as good news. There should be no surprises.
- *Always have cash*. Never ever get close to running out of cash. It's a business-killer.

- *Succeed.* Give yourself the very best chance to enjoy success with flexible and supportive investors. Make sure you always plan for success, right from day one.
- *Enjoy.* Make sure you take time to enjoy the ride and then enjoy the rewards when you reach the destination.

That's it. I wish you every success with your ride on the Money Train and hope this book will help you avoid the mistakes I have seen/made on the way through.

I would just like to repeat that many investments are made by good companies/individuals and lead to success for all.

Hopefully the enabling nature of this book will help you to find those types of relationships, or at least give you some control over the future.

I wish you every success. It's always underestimated how hard it is to set up your own business. If it was easy, everyone would do it, and they don't. Good luck.

PART III

Information

What help and advice do you need, and where do you find it?

I have talked all the way through this book about needing to get the best help and advice that you can to prepare for the fundraising events. You can't know everything, and you can't do everything yourself.

The original reason for putting this book together came when I recognized that young businesses enter the fundraising arena ill-prepared and inexperienced. This is not their fault, just the nature of where the businesses and the founders are in their development.

But they find themselves in a world where all deals are different, and all negotiators have different skills. There is no simple solution to adhere to. The deals can be complicated and multi-layered no matter where in the investment hierarchy you are trying to raise funds.

You don't just need to be a good negotiator; you will also need to understand the complexities of legalese and the levers of the deal. If you don't understand the effect that a clause can have on your business, then no matter how good a negotiator you are, you will get turned over. There will be no escape clause, unless you are really fortunate.

My advice would be to get the best advice you can find/afford. This chapter is to help you go to the right places to find that advice and gives my view on who (or what) are the most important.

When does the need for advice start?

At the very beginning. When you are starting your business, talk to as many other founders as you can about their experiences. They will almost certainly want to share their stories and show off their war wounds. You will find most founders very open to admitting their mistakes and helping you to learn from them. Keep in touch with the ones you find useful. Don't waste their time, though. An occasional cup of tea with a short agenda is usually what works. You don't want to become a chore for them.

Take the time to talk to them about where they got advice from and what was most useful. It will be useful shorthand to help you find the right people and avoid the wrong people.

The externals

Where do you then need to look? First, let's look at the more formal external appointments: lawyers, accountants and advisers.

Lawyers

> Without exception, everyone I spoke to before writing this book said that the right lawyer was the key hiring.

Let's start with lawyers. As I have said in almost every chapter, the most important external hiring is a good lawyer. They will save you from the worst excesses that come your way and will help you make more of your business on whatever measure you use. Without exception, everyone I spoke to before writing this book said that the right lawyer was the key hiring. Here are some individual quotes.

- Founder: 'We really needed someone in our corner'.
- Corporate finance adviser: 'A good lawyer is more important than a good adviser.'
- Founder: 'We learned a bit too late the difference the right lawyer could make'.
- Investor: 'A good lawyer keeps us sharp and doesn't let us take advantage'.
- Founder: 'On our first deal, we had no idea what a deal looked like. Our lawyer made it make sense.'

- Lawyer: 'Deals take a long time. Funds use the time well. Founders run out of energy and steam or interest. They stop being interested and asking questions. They stop being inquisitive. Funds are continually inquisitive. It is our job to fill and bridge those energy gaps.'

For a young business all legal fees look like a lot of money and you very rarely allow for them when raising funds. They always feel like a burdensome cost. A good lawyer is not a cost; it's a very wise investment. In time you will see what a wise investment it is.

> A good lawyer is not a cost; it's a very wise investment. In time you will see what a wise investment it is.

As you grow and the fees look less daunting you can go through the upgrade process. But treat it a little like the house-buying market. Always stretch yourself to the best that you can almost afford. Early on, this is hard. Don't fall into the trap of using your family friend, unless that family friend has the right experience. Do your homework. Talk to some of their clients. Let them take you through some of the deals they have been involved in. Be clear on how they charge. If it's for a defined event, get them to do a fixed price. A good lawyer won't mind you having a good look at their references and charging models.

Talk to other founders and fundraisers about who they would recommend. The lawyer I have worked with for over 25 years came via a recommendation and he has seen me through three exits, a number of fundraises and too many business scrapes to list here.

As you go through the fundraising and the numbers get bigger, don't forget to cost in the legal advice as part of what you need to raise. And don't under-use the lawyer. Get them right into the heart of the negotiation. They are part of your team and your armoury.

Accountants

Let's move onto accountants. I think this group is a little more challenging. Most founders find the word 'accountant' an instant turn-off. Eyes glaze over and they generally say, 'do we really need one of these?' Most lawyers' practices will offer tax advice but most of them will suggest that you hire your own accountant. This is good advice but accountants in the current climate are becoming more and more risk-averse because of increasing scrutiny and regulation.

If we go right back to the early chapters, where we talked about running the company with good governance from an early stage, having someone who gives your numbers the stamp of approval and producing annual accounts is good discipline. At the early stages it isn't a legal requirement to produce full public accounts but it's good discipline to produce the minimum requirement through an accountant. It might seem boring and unnecessary, but it can work for you.

But my advice is to get your accountant working in a narrowly defined space. Let the lawyer give you the broader advice when you need it.

Whilst I have had very few bad experiences with lawyers, I have had rather more poor experiences with accountants. That's why I always suggest that the lawyer takes the lead and guides you through it.

There are three examples here of where accountants have made an impact. First, a start-up I was involved in employed the industry-leading accountants to set the company up. The advice they gave tied up a huge amount of the founder's seed money in the company and we later discovered that we could easily have structured the business so that the initial investment could be taken out, tax-free, when the company was operating profitably. It didn't cost any money, really, but it tied up money for years at a time when the founders were understandably struggling with personal finances.

The second was a business that I made an arm's-length investment in that was doing well and was consistently turning over £3–4 million in revenue. But it just didn't make a profit. I, and a few of the other investors, couldn't understand why this was the case. The company management always seemed to have good reasons as to why this was occurring. After three years of good business and no profits, the arm's-length investors eventually suggested that maybe a forensic accountant should have a detailed look. They looked and found that the CFO had stolen over £1 million from the company – three years' profits. Worryingly, every year the accounts were signed off by the accountancy practice with not a word of concern. The company was reimbursed by the accountants and the bank, and the CFO went to prison. But surely the fraud should have been spotted?

Third, through my motor racing, I am involved in a small racing team and restoration business. I have helped it grow significantly, over 20-fold during the last six to seven years. The accountant is a small local firm but having been involved from day one they know the company well and are always on the lookout for ways to help us. We have put formal finance disciplines in place and have moved to profitability. Having formal accountancy in place and legitimate numbers has improved our credit ratings with suppliers, our reputation with the bank and our qualification for significant, legitimate tax breaks. These include research and development (R&D) tax credits which our accountants suggested that we could qualify for. This has legitimately saved us tens of thousands in tax payments. It has also helped us qualify for ISO9001 listings, in a sector where nobody works to these standards. It's given the company a unique selling point versus the competition.

Why is this important? Because as we worked our way through a global pandemic with no business coming in, we needed to get a loan from the bank to sustain the business. They looked at our financial information and systems and didn't even require personal guarantees to get a loan in place to bridge us through. We used the accountant in a narrow space and they performed really well.

It has been a mix of experiences for me. You need a good accountant and I have a lot of good examples of where they have had a positive effect on the businesses I have worked with. My personal view is that in 99 cases out of 100 a good lawyer is much more important than a good accountant – a point of view that I am sure a lot of accountants would disagree with.

Formal advisers

The final formal group are the advisers. I would categorize these people as being employed to help you with one project. This would exclude non-executive directors or mentors. They will typically be corporate finance partners who specialize in either fundraising or helping you to buy or sell businesses.

They can be a very useful addition to the team as they usually have a wide knowledge of where to look for money or buyers or sellers. There are lots of them. When you are choosing who to work with, the choice usually comes down to trusting an individual, not a company.

I have been involved in businesses that have used a corporate finance company for selling and for raising funds, with mixed results. Their use has been much more successful in the selling of businesses, but less so in fundraising.

It's worth pointing out that these companies are big-ticket items. They usually come with minimum fee levels and they usually start at close to six figures. Choose carefully; make sure you need one in the first place and, if you do, then make sure they are right for you.

Do you need a corporate finance adviser?

Do you need to employ a corporate finance adviser to raise money? If you haven't been doing the fundraising rounds and don't know the market, it may be money well-spent. It's another (big) chunk out of the funds you are raising, though. If you think you can find the right investors yourself, with the help you have, then do it. If you are up against it or have no idea where to go, it could be the lifeline you are looking for.

But don't kid yourself. They don't have a cupboard full of money waiting for you. They will have to go and find it and they will want a lot of work from you to make the investors as interested as possible. And you will spend a lot of time in meetings, many of which will be a waste of time. They will all say that they will do a lot of the work for you, but they can't. You know the business better than they do. The whole process is incredibly distracting and eats up so much time.

Choosing the right one

How do you choose one? It's back to the basics again. Do your homework. Check them out. Talk to people they have worked with before. Get them to show you some successful case histories but also ask them to introduce you to a company where it didn't go all that well.

When making the choice, make sure it's someone you can spend at least two hours in a room with, because you will be doing that a lot. You don't have to love them, but you do need to respect them and their views.

Don't assume that it will end up successfully. Not all corporate finance practices offer a fundraising service, and there is a very good reason for that. It's because they enjoy patchy success in delivering funding, particularly when they are the last-chance saloon for you. Investors can sniff desperation, even in a well-packaged corporate finance wrapper.

If you have the time and you need them for a non-desperate situation, e.g., raising funds in another geography, visit a few or revisit the people you have met on the way through. Trust me, if you have shown any kind of success they will have noticed and got in touch. They may well view the money-raising service as a loss-leader as they make their real money in mergers and acquisitions (M&A). They may help in the short term at a lower fee if you offer them the opportunity to be part of a future sale/purchase.

Some examples

I have had a range of experiences with corporate finance. A couple come to mind. The first was when I was selling a business. It was going to be a big deal, so we decided to use a corporate finance house. We got four corporate finance companies to pitch for our business and set them a range of questions to answer. All were very professional in their response and all of them, unknowingly, helped us work out exactly what we needed. In the end we gave it to the company/individual who was the least like us. Our reasoning was that they would ask all of the difficult questions that we wouldn't know how to ask. It worked and it was part of the reason the transaction was successful.

Less successful was the business that was up against it and needed urgent cash. The chosen corporate finance adviser bounced in like Tigger with a sugar rush. They loved the business and could see lots of investors who would be interested. There were a lot of promises made, but ultimately it just took a lot of time and moved the cash deadline ten weeks closer, with no money in sight. The company was bailed out by its reluctant shareholders, but the over-optimistic promises cost the company time and ultimately the founders negotiating room.

One institutional investor said, 'we prefer not to deal with corporate finance people. Good corporate finance houses are helpful; bad are terrible.' I suspect they were being a little disingenuous. These investors want to get their own way and not be constantly challenged.

But my advice would be to work out what you want the corporate finance adviser for before you engage one. You might find that you don't really need one or that they only need to be in a defined part of the process, as an arm's-length adviser.

> If you can only afford one, then it's a good lawyer every time.

There are other external options, but I have covered the main ones. In the fundraising process, if you can only afford one, then it's a good lawyer every time.

The internals

What about those closer to home, the key advisers that will help guide you through all of your firsts? This would typically be some non-executive help, maybe a chair, a trusted adviser or mentor, industry specialists. I will get to them later, but the first place I want to go is making sure you have some business expertise within the company – most importantly, some finance acumen.

The finance resource

I have covered the need to get a good financial director/CFO/ commercial director on board as soon as you can afford it. They pay for themselves within ten minutes. They represent another investment and not a cost.

> Get a good financial director/CFO/commercial director on board as soon as you can afford it. They pay for themselves within ten minutes.

It's worth listening to what a lawyer I spoke to had to say on this: 'very few entrepreneurial businesses have good general management skills... the cult of CFOs not being trained and experienced is very damaging. Getting a good CFO early pays dividends immediately.' As a founder said to me, 'a great CFO is priceless. Every start-up I know has been too slow to hire one, including us.'

You can see how it happens – or doesn't. As founders of the business you are not likely to be generalists. You are also likely to be at the inexperienced end of the general management experience curve. You don't know what you don't know. But you do know that you are not interested in the things that don't interest you, and cash flow and collecting money are towards the top of that list. Please don't just park it.

If it doesn't interest you, then get someone who it does interest, and get them as fast as the company can afford it – or

> Remember rule number one: don't run out of cash.

at least employ some resource that looks after it. There are plenty of options out there. Remember rule number one: don't run out of cash.

If you have taken money from investors under tax-efficient government schemes, they very often come with criteria that need to be met over a number of years. A good finance person will ensure that you stay in line. They will also help you to avoid paying too much or too little tax. As a lawyer said to me, 'don't be skewered by tax and tax breaks'.

The other benefit is that they will share the load in meeting the requirements of the investors for information. They will become your running mate. It will feel good. The investors will see it as a positive and they will be reassured that someone has an eye on the business. They will focus on the things that bore you. Do make sure that you hold them to account, though. Too much freedom can be very tempting for a misguided CFO.

Advisers

There are thousands of options for getting advisory people on board. They vary enormously in quality, commitment, price and motive. Doing what I do, you won't be surprised to hear that I think experienced advisers can be a key part of your management arsenal – a trusted adviser who has 'been there and done it' and hopefully has learned from all the mistakes they have made on the way through.

But you have to work out what it is you want from these advisers, and it's worth doing that before you start talking to people, mainly because I guarantee that you will change the brief by the time you get to making a decision.

Some of the questions you need to answer include the following.

- Am I looking for sector experience?
- Am I looking for technical experience?
- Do they have to have started their own business?
- Do I want a mentor?
- Do I want someone that comes with money?
- How formal do I want the relationship to be?
- Are we looking for a chair?
- Can I afford to pay?
- Am I looking for a figurehead?
- How much time do I want them for?
- Is this a 'have to have', a 'want to have' or a 'nice to have'?

The list is endless, but you get the drift. It's very hard to give direct advice on the answers, but here are a few thoughts. Being a founder or a CEO is a very lonely place. It's very hard to share the difficult times with either senior staff or investors. There is a very real danger of spooking them. I have found that what some people value is a non-judgemental ear that will listen and give advice. Kick the door shut, unload and try and find a solution. I have been hired as an industry specialist on more than one occasion. Two of those hires have led to chair roles and a much broader mentoring role.

I think one of the key answers is to the question: 'do they have to have started their own business?', particularly for early-stage businesses. The issues are very different to when you are managing a more established business. Again, in my experience founders tend to get more from advisers who have been founders.

How much of their time do I need? You usually get a couple of days a month. The reality is that it should probably be as much or as little time as is required. If it's a chair role and it's fundraising or selling time, then it will be a lot more than that. My view is that you should measure inputs, not time. One five-minute conversation might transform the company.

With regards to a chair, I would advocate maintaining an independent chair for as long as you can, not trying to keep them in your pocket; a good one won't stay in your pocket for very long. But investors tend to have more respect for an independent chair, allowing that chair to operate as a buffer and adviser between the executive and the investors. The relationship between the chair and the founder/CEO is vital, and should be one of mutual respect without dominance from one side.

The chair's role is to represent the best interests of all the shareholders and make sure that the executive team delivers on the agreed strategy. The founder/CEO has to recommend and deliver the strategy and shape the business to deliver it. These are subtle differences in responsibilities.

Whether hiring an adviser or a chair, be very clear on the expectations, and if it's an inexperienced adviser, spend time agreeing the working relationship.

My very first chair role was a voyage of discovery for me and the company. The company had not had a chair before and I hadn't stepped into a company as a non-executive chair before. We agreed one-and-a-half days a month. For the first three months I received an email carefully logging the amount of time I had spent working on the business, with a table showing any deficit or over-delivery of time. After the third email we had a call, and from then on there were no more emails. The gist of our conversation was: 'how much money did that call make/save the company? Is what I am saying not valuable? If all you value is time, then I can come and waste your time if you want me to.' It made the company think, and they then started to use me in a very different way, with lots of short calls and emails and a couple of more formal, face-to-face sessions every month. This actually became the model for my future offer.

One other suggestion would be to commit to a three-month trial. This works really well. It's less commitment and gives both sides the opportunity to get to know each other. If it doesn't work, then you can both move on.

If you do decide to progress, then put in an annual review to make sure it is still a mutually helpful relationship.

A few things to watch out for here.

- There are a lot of non-execs who are still looking to build a CV. Most of these operate in the FTSE corporate world, but some target the hot, leading-edge sectors so that they can show they have 'one of those' on their CV. Few of these are ex-founders, and few of them understand the young business world. They will bring a lot of formality and corporate skills if that is what you want/need.
- Beware the adviser who really wants a full-time role and wants to get involved in the day-to-day of the business. Be very clear on the what, when and how when making the offer. If they become overbearing then push back.
- You might decide you need a figurehead for a couple of reasons. To some people a well-known industry figure or a well-known business name will say that you are serious. The other benefit is that they can often be very acceptable to the

investment community. It can increase the perceived value of the company and can help attract investment interest. If you go down this route, be very clear on what you are getting from them. If they are non-executive/chair of multiple businesses, don't expect too much in the way of attention. I once read of a serial non-executive who was chair of 16 companies. They couldn't possibly pay attention to all of them and, sure enough, a major financial issue was discovered at one of the companies and this figurehead chair had no idea. If you want them to help with raising funds, then make sure they have the time to help you.

I have gone into some of the specifics here but many of these advisers can cover a range of tasks. As you meet people it will become clearer what and who you need. There are thousands of these people available. You can be choosy. Most of these networks work on word of mouth. Ask around. Someone always knows someone.

What about paying for them? If you are very early-stage, some will work for nothing with some equity put on the table. If it's really early, they might also invest in your business. I have done this on several occasions.

If it's a bit later and payment is involved, they will have a view on their own worth but should also have a view on what the company can realistically afford. The range is enormous; it could be in the mid-teens of thousands per annum for a mentor/adviser to anywhere up to a six-figure fee for a heavyweight chair for a later-stage business. Most will expect some equity participation, some of which they may pay for.

Don't be too generous too early, but do make sure their value is reflected as time goes on. Keep an eye on it. It's very easy to forget to review.

Really good advisers/non-executives can make huge material differences to young businesses, particularly through tough times, and not just materially; they can also be the calm guide and personal mentor to get you through the emotional rollercoasters.

The board member/adviser from the investor

It's unlikely that a chair will be imposed on the company by the investor in the early rounds of investment. But if the investment is a significant one then it is likely that a board representative will be part of the deal. If it's an individual investor, then obviously it's hard to have any choice in who it is. However, if the investment is from venture capital or somebody to represent a number of small investors then make sure you have some choice in who it is. Having someone who turns up to the board trying to trip either the management or the company up is not a great place to be and will make the board meetings divisive and unproductive.

One thing to remember is that the board member representing the investor is, as a finance adviser said to me, 'a walking conflict of interest'. They are representing the money and protecting that money. They will give good advice around this but all of their advice (and votes) will be informed by this position, sometimes against the best interest of the company.

Keep your options open and, as one corporate finance adviser said to me, 'if there is a choice of non-executive to be had make sure you have that choice'.

I had an odd experience when negotiating an investment deal. I was chair of the company trying to raise the funds. The negotiation got around to board representation. It was a big investment and they wanted a board seat and an observer seat (basically, someone who could come to the board meeting and observe, with no voting rights and no voice – although it never works out that way and they always seem to find their voice!). All of this was fine.

It then came to the chair role. They wanted the right to appoint the next chair and at a timing of their choice. Keeping my 'what's best for the company' hat on, I argued the point that the company should try to find the next chair, not have one imposed. This was not to protect my own position or to ensure that a weak chair would be installed as my successor. A strong chair is vital. It was to try and ensure that the relationship of mutual respect with the CEO was maintained. In the end they agreed to the company being able to put forward three candidates with approval 'not unreasonably withheld'. As it happened, the raise didn't go ahead, but this was another addition to the learning pool.

Just to demonstrate how badly it can go, a corporate finance adviser gave me an example of a poor decision. It was a private equity investment, but it makes the point. 'The founder and the imposed chair were chalk and cheese. The founder was from the north and state-educated; the chairman was from the south and privately educated. The chair thought it was the investors' company and the founder thought (rightly) it was theirs, or certainly theirs to run. After a lot of falling out the founder was fired and some months later the company collapsed. Everybody lost.' A perfectly good, successful business went under because of some bad miscasting. Keep as much choice as you possibly can.

This chapter is mainly about getting the right help. The most important thing is to work out what help you need or might need. Before that you need to acknowledge that help is needed in the first place. That is quite often difficult to do if you are consumed with the day-to-day. It is amazing how quickly you can get used to the norm or putting off something you haven't got the first idea how to solve. Good help is priceless. Listen to your peers and they will generally point you in the right direction. As I said earlier, there are thousands of options out there; just make sure you get the right casting.

All aboard the Money Train: What help and advice do you need, and where do you find it?

- There is a lot of help to be had, and that help is available and willing to give advice. Talk to other founders to point you in the right direction.

- Work out what help you need and ask for it.

- First, get the best lawyer you can afford and upgrade as time goes on. It's an investment, not a cost.

- Second, get a finance function in place. Don't leave it too late. It's another investment, not another cost.

- Individual advisers can help you personally and professionally. Work out what you need them for and take your time to choose them.

- Beware the adviser who wants to try and dominate the business.

- Beware the figurehead adviser with limited time.

- Use a trial period to see if the casting is right.

- Maintain an independent chair for as long as you can.

- If an investor imposes a board member, try and get a choice or a right of veto.

Abbreviations, information, resources and jargon

At the start of the book I mentioned that the world of investment is full of jargon. When you first enter these discussions, it can sound like a completely different language. In the book I have tried to use the full terms to make it easier to understand. To help things along, in this section I have listed some of the terms you will come across, what they mean and, where appropriate, how they are referred to.

I have also tried to put the terms into groups to help with the understanding.

Investors

Seed investors

Seed money, sometimes known as seed funding or seed capital, is a form of funding offering in which an investor invests capital in a start-up company in exchange for an equity stake in the company. This is usually before the company is up and running. They are sometimes known as 'friends and family investors', even when they aren't!

Angel investors

An angel investor is an individual who provides financial backing for small start-ups or entrepreneurs, typically in exchange for ownership equity in the company. Often, angel investors are found amongst an entrepreneur's family and friends. They are referred to as 'angels'.

High-net-worths

A high-net-worth individual is somebody with significant liquid financial assets. They are similar to angels but have more money and are also potential clients for the venture capital and private equity funds.

Angel investor networks

An angel investor network is a group of angels who invest collectively, allowing them to operate more effectively and provide mutual support. Angel network members meet for presentations from entrepreneurs, after which they review the business proposals and make decisions on investments. Often known as 'angel networks'.

Venture capital funds

Venture capital funds are investment funds that manage the money of investors who seek private equity stakes in start-up and small to medium-sized enterprises with strong growth potential. These investments are generally characterized as high-risk/high-return opportunities. Often referred to as 'VCs'.

Venture capital trust funds

A venture capital trust fund (in the UK) is a company that has been approved by the tax authorities and invests in, or lends money to, unlisted companies. There are limits to the companies these funds can invest in; the size of investment and length of trading time are the two main criteria. Often referred to as 'VCTs'.

Private equity funds

Private equity funds raise money from institutions and wealthy individuals and then invest that money in buying and selling businesses. After raising a specified amount, a fund will close to new investors; each fund is liquidated, selling all its businesses, within a pre-set time frame, usually no more than ten years. Often referred to as 'PEs'.

Financial terms

Annual recurring revenue

Annual recurring revenue refers to the monetary value of a subscription-based company's subscriber base or the yearly value of a single subscription. This metric is most often used to measure yearly revenue for subscription services. Also known as 'ARR'.

Monthly recurring revenue

Monthly recurring revenue measures the total amount of predictable revenue that a company expects on a monthly basis. MRR is an important figure for tracking monthly revenue figures and to understand the month-to-month differences if you have a subscription service. Also known as 'MRR'.

Cash flow

Cash flow is the net amount of cash and cash equivalents being transferred into and out of a business. At the most fundamental level, a company's ability to create value for shareholders is determined by its ability to generate positive cash flows, i.e., more coming in than going out. Referred to as 'really really important'!

Cash burn and cash runway

The cash burn rate is used by start-up companies and investors to track the amount of monthly cash that a company spends before it starts generating its own income. A company's burn rate is also used as a measuring stick for its cash runway, which is the amount of time the company has before it runs out of money.

So, if a company has £100,000 in the bank and it spends £10,000 a month, its burn rate would be £10,000 and its runway would be ten months. Usually referred to as simply 'burn' and 'runway'.

Profit terms

You will be exposed to a lot of terms around profit. Amongst them will be:

- gross profit
- net profit
- EBIT
- EBITDA

There are a thousand business websites that will give you the definition of these ways of measuring profit. All you need to know is that these are profit descriptors. Get your finance expert to explain what they are. If they can't explain these clearly and easily, then you have the wrong person.

Legal terms

Articles of association

The articles of association form a document that specifies the regulations for a company's operations and defines the company's purpose. The document lays out how tasks are to be accomplished within the organization, including the process for appointing directors and the handling of financial records. It is a document that protects the company and is referred to as the 'articles'.

Shareholders' agreement

A shareholders' agreement is an arrangement amongst the company's shareholders that describes how the company should be operated.

It outlines shareholders' rights and obligations. It protects the shareholders. This agreement can sometimes override the articles and sometimes it's the other way around.

Preference shares

Preference shares are shares in a company that are owned by people who have the right to receive part of the company's profits before the holders of ordinary shares are paid. They also have the right to have their investment repaid if the company sells or fails and has to close. Also known as 'prefs'.

Loan notes

A loan note is a contract for a loan stating when the loan must be repaid, and the interest that's payable. It can also contain additional provisions such as convertibility into equity (shareholding) or other types of debt – in which case it's called a 'convertible loan note'.

Investor consent

Investor consent is a right that requires the approval of the investors (typically defined as all shareholders other than the founders) for a range of key company decisions that could affect the value of the investors' investments.

Intellectual property

Intellectual property refers to creations of the mind, such as inventions; literary and artistic works; designs; and symbols, names and images used in commerce.

Intellectual property is usually protected in law by patents, copyright and trademarks. This makes sure that people/companies earn recognition or financial benefit from what they invent or create. Known as 'IP'.

Warranties

Warranties are representations made by the warrantors, who are usually the founders, and the company that certain statements relating to the company are true and accurate at the completion date.

A really helpful resource

BVCA

In their own words, 'The British Private Equity & Venture Capital Association (BVCA) is the industry body for the private equity and venture capital industry in the UK. With more than 750 member firms – including over 325 fund managers and 125 institutional investors – it is our role to inform and engage, to demonstrate the positive role of our industry in the UK economy and provide market intelligence, technical updates, specialist training and more.' The BVCA also has a huge range of sample documents that you might come across in your investment rounds with PEs and VCs. Visit www.bvca.co.uk.

Deal terms and words

Sweat equity

The term 'sweat equity' refers to a person or company's contribution towards a business venture or other project. Sweat equity is generally not monetary and, in most cases, comes in the form of the original idea, physical and mental input and time. Sweat equity is commonly found in start-up share structures.

Due diligence

Due diligence is a comprehensive appraisal of a business undertaken by a prospective buyer, especially to establish its assets and liabilities and to evaluate its commercial potential. Often known as 'DD'.

Investment committee

The term 'investment committee' refers to a fund's committee that will oversee, advise and consult with respect to the fund's investment strategy. It will make the final decision on whether an investment will be made. Often known as the 'IC'.

Data rooms

Data rooms are spaces used for housing data, usually of a secure or privileged nature. They can be physical data rooms, virtual data rooms or data centres. They are used for a variety of purposes, including data storage, document exchange, file sharing, financial transactions, legal transactions and more.

Share dilution

Share dilution (also known as equity dilution) occurs when a company issues new shares resulting in a decrease of an existing shareholder's ownership percentage of that company. Share dilution can also occur when holders of share options, such as company employees, exercise their share options. When the number of shares increases, each existing stockholder owns a smaller, or diluted, percentage of the company, making each share less valuable. Often simply called 'dilution'.

Retained equity

Retained equity is rarely used but usually refers to a situation where people that are leaving the business retain their shareholding. This usually happens if they are seen as a good leaver and almost always comes with a very limited list of things they can do with the shares.

Geography

For some reason, the sector never refers to another country as a market. It is always called a geography.

Examples of tax-efficient schemes in the UK

These schemes vary around the world but the schemes in the UK that are most relevant to investors are listed below. I have taken some of the words from the UK government website (www.gov.uk). It is probably worth checking as the details on these schemes do change constantly.

Seed Enterprise Investment Scheme (SEIS)

SEIS is designed to help your company raise money when it's starting to trade. It does this by offering tax relief to investors who buy new shares in your company. It's a fairly limited level of investment and it has to happen early in the life of the company, but because it is seen as risky then the tax reliefs going in are instant and very good. There are also very attractive tax treatments on exit.

The company has to remain SEIS-compliant for three years after the investment for the tax reliefs on the investment and on the benefits at sale to be fully realized.

Enterprise Investment Scheme (EIS)

EIS is designed so that your company can raise money to help grow your business. It does this by offering tax reliefs to individual investors who buy new shares in your company.

Under EIS, you can raise a lot more money and a lot later into the life of your business than under SEIS. As a result, the tax benefits are still generous, but less generous than with SEIS.

You must follow the scheme rules so that your investors can claim and keep EIS tax reliefs relating to their shares. Tax reliefs will be withheld or withdrawn from your investors if you do not follow the rules for at least three years after the investment is made.

Share options (EMI)

Whilst not strictly applicable to the investors, the awarding of share options will ultimately have a diluting effect on the investors' shareholding and therefore the value of their investment.

Enterprise Management Incentive (EMI) schemes are very tax-efficient for employees and employers and are therefore very popular. Again, you should look at the website to get the current details.

If you work for a company with assets of £30 million or less, it may be able to offer EMIs. Your company can grant you share options up to the value of £250,000 in a three-year period.

You won't have to pay income tax or National Insurance if you buy the shares for at least the market value they had when you were granted the option. There are also some very good tax breaks on any profit made from these options.

General market terms

Bull market

A bull market is the condition of a financial market in which prices are rising or are expected to rise. The term 'bull market' is most often used to refer to the stock market but can be used in the investment market if there is a lot of money around and not much to buy. Often referred to as 'bullish'.

Bear market

A bear market is when a market experiences prolonged price decline. It typically describes a condition in which stock market prices fall 20% or more from recent highs amidst widespread pessimism and negative investor sentiment. In the investment market it is when there isn't much money around and a lot of companies looking for funding. Often referred to as 'bearish'.

Unicorn business

A unicorn business is a term used in the venture capital/private equity world to describe a privately held start-up company with a value of over $1 billion. It's often just called a 'unicorn' and it's a very good target to aim to become one of these!

Mergers and acquisitions

A merger occurs when two separate entities combine forces to create a new, joint organization. An acquisition refers to the takeover of one entity by another. Mergers and acquisitions may be completed to expand a company's reach or gain market share in an attempt to create shareholder value. Often just called 'M&A'.

About the author

For the first 15 years of my career I worked in a variety of advertising agencies.

I found my first job in 1974 – like the rest of the 1970s, a year of considerable industrial strife. The oil crisis of 1973 and the imposition of a three-day week through a coal miners' strike in 1974 meant that there were very few jobs around anywhere.

I managed to get a job offer in the second-largest agency in the country, working in media. It was rather grandly called Masius, Wynne-Williams and D'Arcy Macmanus. My job was to negotiate pricing and place ads on television on behalf of clients.

The 1980s were a very good time to work in advertising, a hard-working industry with good rewards. I did well. I became a main board director of an agency called WCRS at the age of 29 and part of an executive board running the agency at 31. It was during this period that I met my future business partner. We became a proper team and with one other partner left WCRS to start our own business. We had no clients and no income; it was scary. That business was called PHD and is now an Omnicom-owned worldwide media business operating in over 80 countries.

From start-up, the business enjoyed considerable success and we sold it after six years. We delivered on a five-year earn-out, during which I attended an advanced management programme at Harvard Business School. Having not been to university, I saw it as university with a gold card. Fortunately, it was someone else's gold card, which made it all the more pleasurable.

After the earn-out I then moved to New York to set up the PHD US office across seven cities. I lived there for three years, returned to the UK and then travelled the world, opening offices in Moscow, Warsaw, Dubai, Singapore, Hong Kong, Kuala Lumpur and many more.

After 17 years of growing a business and seven years after the earn-out, I left the company I had founded. I had done every job there was to do and left as a good leaver. Wondering what to do next, I was approached to become the CEO of a very successful digital media business. This was in the early days of the digital media industry. This was a bubble business that was right for the times but was unlikely to maintain its competitive edge indefinitely. The founders and investors wanted it sold and they wanted me to do it for them. I had sold a business I had founded, but returning to working for founders and selling on their behalf was a new experience for me.

The company went through a complete corporate finance run process and was sold a month before the world economic crisis in June 2008. In hindsight it looks like genius planning, but actually it was just very good luck. A few years later, the crisis was part of the reason that the bubble burst, but at sale time the founders and investors made a lot of money. For a number of years this was the biggest digital deal in the sector.

Having sold the business, I moved to a non-executive chair role, and that was the starting point of the next phase of my career. I moved from being a full-time executive to a range of roles as non-executive, chairman, mentoring, advising and helping, becoming a 'wingman' to watch the backs of founders, CEOs and companies. It wasn't planned and to be honest I thought I would move on to another executive role, but the opportunities decided that a new career path was the route forward.

For this whole period my criteria for getting involved in a business have been simple and have remained the same.

- Can I spend two hours in a room with these people?
- Is it an interesting product/service?
- Can I make a difference?

I have chaired a lot of boards, mainly of young businesses but with some established companies as well, acting as a guide and wise counsel. Some have been difficult, some a joy and some both at the same time.

I have worked in a range of industries such as advertising, marketing, publishing, construction, motorsport, AdTech, MarTech,

FinTech, production and broadcasting. This has given me a very wide range of experience in the digital space.

In addition, I have taken the role of an angel investor, have been a mentor to CEOs of big companies and have been part of start-up teams and stayed for the whole journey to successful exit. I have helped CEOs restructure companies, sort out cash flow issues and complete mergers and acquisitions. I have been an enabler with introductions and doors opened in my network. It's been a joy working with some very smart people and seeing them succeed.

And of course, I have watched, led or added a light touch to young, growing businesses who are looking to raise money for their next stage of development. Other than setting up a business in the first place, it is without doubt the most stressful, time-consuming and distracting part of a young company's development.

And that is why I decided to write this book, to try and help young businesses navigate their way through this really hard process. I hope it has been useful and you enjoyed the read.

www.davidpattison.com
wingman@davidpattison.com